OUT OF BOUNDS

PIPER

East Coast
NEW YORK CITY

Executive Offices
BLUE EARTH, MN 56013

West Coast
SAN FRANCISCO

OUT OF BOUNDS

AN ANECDOTAL HISTORY OF NOTRE DAME FOOTBALL

Michael Bonifer
L. G. Weaver

Manufactured in the United States of America.

International Standard Book Number: 0-87832-043-1

Library of Congress Catalog Card Number: 78-60060

First Edition, First Printing

Library of Congress Cataloging in Publication Data

Bonifer, Michael.
    Out of bounds.

    1. Notre Dame, Ind. University--History--
Anecdotes, facetiae, satire, etc. 2. Football
players--United States--Biography. 3. Football
coaches--United States--Biography--Anecdotes,
facetiae, satire, etc. I. Weaver, L. G.,
joint author. II. Title.
GV958.N6B66   796.33'2'0922 [B] 78-60060
ISBN 0-87832-043-1

Table of Contents

Dedication

To Our Parents

Photo Credits

Thanks to the Notre Dame Sports Information Department, Notre Dame International Sports & Games Research Collection, The Dome, Bagby Studios, Knute Rockne Jr., Herb Eggert, Mario Tonelli, Zenon Bidzinski, Bruce Harlan, and Rex Lobo.

Special thanks to Chris Smith, a talented and savvy professional.

Reminiscing

by
Edward "Moose" Krause

The Jack Dempsey — Jess Willard title fight held on July 4, 1919 in Toledo, Ohio, was the first major sporting event I ever attended. It was an experience that has been indelibly impressed on my mind since that memorable day.

I was six years old at the time and I remember the event primarily for two reasons: This was my first train trip and I recall Dempsey, a little guy at 195, defeating a mammoth Jess Willard.

It was because of a little player that I received my nickname "Moose" while playing football as a sophomore at DeLaSalle High School in Chicago. My coach and close friend, Judge Norman Barry, a teammate of the Gipper's — seeing the trouble I was having blocking the little guy — yelled at me, "You're big enough to be a Moose and you can't even block a little guy."

I was the first player to have that nickname and it's followed me throughout my career. There have been others — Moose Fischer and Moose Connor who later made All-American at Notre Dame, but I have the "honor" of being number one.

There was one game in particular during my playing days at Notre Dame that stands out in my memory. This was the Army game in 1933. The Cadets were favored by about thirty points. The Irish played their hearts out and we won 13-12. That day I managed to deflect, not block cleanly, about eight punts. These deflections so shook up the Army that they changed formations and started putting two players in their backfield on punt formations. Their job was to block our great end, Wayne Millner, and me.

Late in the game we were behind by a touchdown and Army went into punt formation. Wayne and I set up a play. At the snap I ran in, jumped over the first back, grabbed the second and all three of us went down in a heap. Millner blocked the punt with his knees — he had so much time to get in. The ball

bounced into the end zone where Jim Harris and I fell on it. We were both holding the ball but the officials gave the touchdown to Harris.

I never scored a pointed in my college career but I always maintained that three of those six points should have been credited to me.

There were some memorable occasions when I returned to Notre Dame as a coach. I handled the team a few times when Frank Leahy was ill, once at USC in 1946. I gave the team a rousing pep talk before the game and I topped it off by pointing at the door and shouting, "Now get out there and beat 'em!" The team was on its way out of the dressing room when Lujack came up to me and told me I'd forgotten to name a starting line-up. "Everybody starts!" I shouted. I was the most excited person in that dressing room. Somehow we got eleven

people on the field, and we absolutely clobbered the Trojans, 26-6. That victory clinched a National Championship for us.

Being at the University of Notre Dame all these years has been a singular honor for me. I have had the privilege of being associated with three men whom I consider legends — Rockne, Leahy, and Parseghian. In a word, I have found my career at the school of Our Lady to be extremely rewarding and replete with fine memories.

Many of those memories are included in *Out of Bounds*. I'm very impressed with this book. I'm sure every football fan will find it informative and interesting.

Ed "Moose" Krause

Edward W. "Moose" Krause grew up back of the stockyards on Chicago's South Side. From DeLaSalle High School he went to Notre Dame, where he has been a big man on the sports scene for nearly half a century. His collegiate athletic career, the stuff of legend, saw him letter in three sports and gain All-America honors in both football and basketball. After brief coaching stints at St. Mary's (Minnesota) and Holy Cross, Krause returned to Notre Dame as football line coach and head basketball coach. In 1949 he was appointed athletic director, a position he has held for nearly thirty years. He is a member of the National Basketball Hall of Fame and has been named Man of the Year by the Walter Camp Hall of Fame.

Introduction

"Yeah, but listen, are you sure you wanna talk to *me?*"

That was the usual question, the almost inevitable query of every ex-bench warmer and forgotten reserve we contacted; even some still brightly shining stars had no idea why we wanted to interview them for our book.

It was not easy to explain to men who were often dimly suspicious that our spiel might end in a pitch for the University growth fund. It was back in February of 1977 that we came up with the notion of writing an offbeat history of Notre Dame football. Ours would avoid everything all the others depended on. Scores, statistics, "crucial" games, winners and losers — all had been reported *ad nauseam*. We wanted to offer something new: a book focusing on the human element, the personalities, the humor, the unusual. Most importantly, while researching Notre Dame's already thoroughly documented past, we decided to base our manuscript on interviews we conducted ourselves, not the usual faded newspaper clippings and rehashed game accounts that were the fodder of most Notre Dame football books.

The idea seemed uncomplicated enough. But sixteen months, several thousand miles, over two hundred interviews, and reams of watermarked bond later, we realized why all the other books were written as they had been. Locating and interviewing former Fighting Irish who were scattered across the country proved to be a slow and sometimes tedious task. There were several false starts during which family and friends anxiously counseled us to throw up the whole scheme and try to catch on somewhere as junior executives, or, failing that, fry cooks. We had compiled a long list of people we wanted to see, but getting to them was another matter entirely,

especially by the Winter of 1978, when howling, monster blizzards buried us whenever we ventured out with notebooks and tape recorder.

At any rate, the interviews were gradually ticked off. We talked to coaches, managers, fans, anyone who had been close to the Notre Dame football program and wanted to share his recollections. But mostly we talked to the players — any players — from Heisman Trophy winners to guys who never made it past the training table.

We wanted to interview everybody. Our theory, which held up a lot longer than we have, is that the forgotten men — the ones who make practices and sidelines and road trips interesting — enhance the character and tradition of Notre Dame football as much as the big heroes. Indeed, we were squeezing in interrogations up to the day we shipped the manuscript to Piper Publishing, five or six "deadlines" later.

Some of the old gridders could simply not remember a single amusing anecdote from their playing years, much as they tried. Others cornered us in their offices or living rooms or kitchens and showered stories on us till we ached with writers' cramp and excess laughter. And every so often, we'd hit the mother lode: a person with a photographic memory. While these rare birds were invaluable to our research, there was the constant problem of steering them into pertinent areas of information and away from such topics as the college board scores of the 1938 jayvee team.

★ ★ ★

A few of our adventures still return in chronic flashbacks. We are at the Notre Dame library with Chet Grant, sports historian emeritus at the University, teammate of the Gipper's, bowlegged and spry as an eighty-year-old man can be. Mr.

Grant is trying to teach us the mechanics of the Notre Dame shift as Rockne had taught it to him. He positions us at the halfback spots, takes his stance at quarterback, and we march self consciously through the steps as several students stare through the big plate glass windows, wondering what kind of weird religion this is where the two young acolytes are chanting and dancing with the little yogi. Grant is immune to such attention. He is watching us and criticizing our technique: "No, no! You've got to bring your left arm across like this . . . plant the foot, pause, then move with the snap . . . Again . . . Hike! . . . One, two, three . . . go!" It's bad enough that we weren't fit for stardom in our own college years, but Mr. Grant's dissatisfaction with our performance leaves us with the humbling realization that we couldn't have made the 1915 freshman team.

Then there was the interview with the stout ex-pro footballer who insisted that we sit in a saloon and throw down drinks at his own suicidal rate. What did we talk about? Who knows? Hours later, we reeled out of the bar forgetting even where we had parked the car.

One of the highlights of our research was the discovery of Knute Rockne's briefcase, noteworthy not only for its value to our project, but as an important artifact in the history of college football. The event caught us completely off guard. The man being interviewed told us he might have a few items in his garage that would interest us. We had become somewhat blase about people who claimed to have interesting items in garages, and half-expected the fellow to strut back into the room with a shoelace once worn by Frank Carideo, or something of the sort. When he showed us the old brown leather case bulging with the legendary coach's personal papers, we were dumbfounded. After sorting through it we hinted that we wanted to return at a later date to re-examine the contents. "Just take the whole thing with you," we were told. A stroke of good fortune made up for dozens of interviews where the subjects sat mainly mute.

★ ★ ★

We think you'll like the blend here, a combination of new material, a few irresistable old chestnuts, a benchful of players ranging from the cream of the roster to the crumbs. Be mindful that the anecdotes in this book don't necessarily reflect a person's character. They are merely vignettes from a long and colorful history, stories you'd likely hear at a reunion of teams past, the oddball sidelights that stay in a player's memory long after scores have been forgotten. Remember also that reminiscences are made to be enjoyed, not authenticated. All of these stories were presented to us in strict sincerity, but the football memory tends to embellish as years go by. After all, only half the lies the Irish tell are true.

Collaboration raises the impossible question: Who wrote what? The only answer is that we both wrote everything, several times. We reworked each other's stories, edited, argued, fought, appeased, surrendered, and double-crossed each other ferociously. And for better or worse the finished product is not his and mine, but *ours*.

Obviously, we could never have completed the book without sturdy support from the sidelines. Herb Juliano and Chet Grant shepherded us through the Notre Dame International Sports and Games Research Collection. Kim and Jeannie in Notre Dame Sports Information managed to cope with our frequent tantrums. The immortal Zenon Bidzinski offered free legal advice that we ignored and expensive camera equipment that we did not know how to use and tried hard not to break. Chris

Smith, a darkroom wizard, printed many of the photographs in this book from the authors' badly botched negatives. Tom Gillespie, Colonel Jack Crowley, Greg Gramelspacher, the D. C. Callaghans, and the folks at St. Pat's helped us keep our personal lives in their normal state of disarray. Bob Fanning Jr., our earliest supporter, lent his assistance in a multitude of ways. And we could never properly thank the hundreds of footballers who so generously and good naturedly shared their time and memories. Without them, there would be no book.

There were others, too, who helped keep the ball rolling. Thanks. You're all invited over for pizza.

L. G. Weaver

Michael Bonifer

July, 1978

A Note About the Authors

Weaver

L. G. Weaver was born and raised in Coshocton, Ohio, in the rolling, strip mine scarred foothills of the Appalachians. He holds a bachelor's degree in English from the University of Notre Dame, and is a member of Phi Beta Kappa, the honorary fraternity. He has become a regular around the frat house, hazing plebes and teaching the secret handshake.

Weaver's lifelong interest in poetry dimmed when he realized there were no long term contracts available in the field. His published verse could be anthologized on a matchbook.

Likewise, his enthusiasm for politics has availed him nothing, perhaps because of his penchant for backing sure losers. He once held a politically appointed position with the Ohio Highway Department, where he washed trucks and swept garages.

A classically trained pianist, Weaver will, if requested, trip through his repertoire: "Summertime" and six bars of "On the Meadow." He enjoys drawing pictures, but often has trouble explaining what they are.

Out of Bounds is L. G. Weaver's first book; great things are expected of him.

Front Row: TV set, Weaver, refreshments, Bonifer.

Bonifer

Michael Bonifer grew up on a farm in Ireland (Ireland, Indiana, that is — population 300) where his family dabbled in everything from a riding stable to tomato growing. Born on New Year's Eve, 1953, he was the oldest of six children.

The author attended high school in Jasper, Indiana ("Nation's Wood Furniture Capital"), where he played basketball for the Wildcats, tennis for the Wildcats, and was a drum major in the Wildcat Marching Band. In the fall of 1971 he enrolled at Notre Dame. Four years later he found himself with a degree in Marketing and a job with a large, multi-national corporation. For a brief time he oiled the gears of big business, then in 1977 decided to pursue a long-time interest — writing.

Out of Bounds is Bonifer's first book. He is now testing the shark-infested waters of network television writing in Los Angeles.

I.
For the Fun of It
1887-1917

Why did you annually spend one May day of your adolescence buying your mother satin-wrapped coat hangers and perfumed guest soap? For Mother's Day, of course. And whom do you blame for that? Why, Francis E. Hering, Notre Dame's first full-time football coach. Of course.

On February 7, 1904, six years after he had resigned as the Notre Dame coach, Hering addressed the national convention of the Fraternal Order of Eagles at the English Opera House in Indianapolis. Hering's harangue, "Our Mothers and Their Importance in Our Lives," was the opening salvo in his campaign to institute Mother's Day. Ten years later, a brief interlude by government standards, Congress took action and Hering had his wish. Florists and candy makers all over America should have his picture hanging on their walls.

Back to Hering's remarkable football career. After quarterbacking the University of Chicago squad in 1893 and 1894, Hering surfaced as coach of the Bucknell Bisons; he probably played for the Bisons as well, under an assumed name. By 1896, Hering had landed the Notre Dame coaching job. Following accepted practice under the era's hazy eligibility rules, Hering was also team captain, starring at a number of positions. Besides all that, he found time to teach English and study law; and he actually collected part of his pay in cuts of beef from the Notre Dame farm.

Hering brought the team its first regional recognition. Schools such as Indiana, Purdue, Illinois and Michigan State were coaxed into the schedule for the first time, while Chicago and Michigan returned from a few years' absence. Despite the tougher opponents, the Blue and Gold managed to win two-thirds of its games. People were beginning to get the idea that the boys from South Bend could play football with the best of them.

In later years, Frank Hering and a friend.

Coaching was a young man's game in those days. Hering left after the 1898 season and a three year record of 12-6-1. He continued bumping heads in pro ball for years, worked as a magazine editor, and in later life published a volume of poetry. Nor did he neglect his pet project: staking a spot on the calendar for mom. Notre Dame soon had the rare distinction of being coached by the Father of Mother's Day.

Now, when's the last time you gave your mom an autographed football?

★ ★ ★

When Mike Daly booted Notre Dame's first field goal on November 6, 1897, more than one of the opposing Chicago Maroons had no idea what was happening. It was the first "Princeton style" place kick west of Pennsylvania.

The game seems so immutable to us now. Back then football changed with the seasons. Rules were dropped or added or switched around. Everyone felt free to tinker; the growing game fed on the energy of innovation.

Let's backtrack a bit. Most historians pin a birthdate of 1869 on the grand old game, but football in those days was little more than rugby gone wild. European rules were ignored; American rules did not exist.

The true dawn of modern football came in 1880 when Yale's Walter Camp introduced a game that featured a scrimmage with undisputed ball possession. This elimated the scrum, which resembled a can-can line turning against itself, the players bowing in a big circle and kicking at the ball and each other's shins while pushing in the general direction of the opponent's goal line. Camp's new rules freed a team to plan and occasionally even execute an attack, instead of depending on a haphazard mad dash for the goal line when the ball finally popped out of the scrum. Camp also limited the number of players to eleven on a side. Schools had been playing with anywhere from thirty to fifty to one hundred on the field at once, the resulting contests looking like strange and dangerous Easter egg hunts.

★

Standardized scoring began in 1883. It allowed two points for a touchdown, four for a point after (that's no misprint), and two for a safety. A year later, the awards for a TD and PAT were reversed. Field goals were worth five.

The early game consisted of two thirty minute "innings." Sixty minutes of action, quartered, did not begin until 1909. Originally, the offense was given three downs to either gain ten yards or lose five . . . you figure it. By 1912, teams had the familiar four downs for ten yards, and scoring values were identical to today's (except for the two-point conversion, which showed up in 1957). By the way, it was not unusual for teams to mutually agree on a reduction of game time if one squad had to catch an early train home, or if the contest was an obvious mismatch.

★

Wedge plays were common in those early days. The offensive team closed in tightly around the ball carrier, arranging themselves like bowling pins. Each man grabbed the waist of the man in front and shoved, and the human battering ram was on its way.

The defense usually stopped the wedge by choosing a human sacrifice who would, willy-nilly, toss himself in front of the lead blocker and pile up the play. At least that was the idea. Even when it worked, a stalled wedge was no problem. The ball carrier was simply hoisted and hurled over the line. Keep in mind, these guys were doing all this to relax and have fun.

Near the turn of the century, chunky tackles and guards started to slip into the backfield, beefing up the wedge and giving the attack more of a knockout punch. This was all going on in the days of mass momentum — players started running before the ball was hiked.

Sound dangerous? It was. There were eighteen deaths and almost one hundred and fifty serious injuries in the 1905 season alone. By 1910, the wedge, flying block and tackle, and other literally bone-crunching plays had been legislated out of existence.

★

This left the door open for the passing attack. Sort of. In fact, the pass had to work its way up like a Horatio Alger hero. In 1906, forward passing was legalized with these provisos: a ball passed out of bounds or striking the ground without being touched, reverted to the opponent; a pass touched but not held was treated as a fumble; any pass over the goal line was a touchback; passing was illegal if done within five yards of where the ball was put into play. By the time a quarterback memorized these rules, the season was usually over.

By 1909, a pass could cross the line of scrimmage at any point, but the toss had to be less than twenty yards to be allowed. By 1912, the twenty yard limit went the way of the wedge. A ball could also be passed over the goal line with the simple requirement that it be caught. If not, a touchback resulted. The end zone was actually invented in 1912 so that receivers would have a defined area in which to snag a forward pass.

The spiral pass, by most accounts, was discovered by accident. When passing was legalized, rulesmakers assumed the ball would be shoveled underhanded or flipped end-over-end to the receiver. A few months later, Coach E. B. Cochems of St. Louis University spotted one of his players tossing spirals before practice. Delighted, Coach Cochems assembled his team for a demonstration. "We'll call it the overhead-projectile-spiral pass," beamed Cochrems, displaying a flair for inflated phrases that would win him a university fellowship today.

seen hiking spirals during punting practice. Intrigued Irish backs floated a few experimental forward spirals. They worked. The spiral was in South Bend to stay.

★

Even as new offensive opportunities unfolded, teams approached the game with the same attitude as the girls we used to date in high school. It was defense, defense, defense. The watchword was beware. Any suggestion of taking a chance was scowled at, nastily.

The game's simple strategy often consisted of keeping the ball in the opponent's territory and waiting for a fumble or a blocked punt. To this end, teams that won the toss almost always elected to kick off, a phenomenon as rare today as the nickel beer. First down punts were frequent and virtually standard procedure for a team caught behind its own twenty yard line. Most coaches treated the forward pass like a short-fused stick of dynamite, allowing their players to throw it only in cases of extreme emergency. Plodding, straight-ahead

power football was the order of the day.

Substitution was rare. The rules flipflopped here and there, but you can basically figure that any player leaving the game could not return until the beginning of the next quarter. The eleven men on the field handled offensive and defensive chores as well as the kicking game. Platoon football and player specialization are relatively recent developments. Ballplayers of the early era were ironmen all.

★ ★ ★

Just how important are coaches, anyway? The 1901 team had two, Pat O'Dea and Jim McWeeney. Perhaps that was two too many. McWeeney, a heavyweight wrestler and future South Bend Police Chief, was a tough, bruising blowhard. He liked to advise ballcarriers to "go into the line with your free fist doubled." O'Dea, smaller and younger, had considered it a bit of a coup when he got Wisconsin to schedule Notre Dame in 1900. Sometimes, scheduling over your head backfires, as O'Dea discovered when the Badgers chewed up the small-potatoes Irish, 54-0.

The two coaches grew to be bitter rivals, fighting over the team like jealous suitors. Relations were so sour between them that, during scrimmages, hefty McWeeney often dug in against players partial to O'Dea. Since O'Dea was supposed to be the head coach and McWeeney his trusted assistant, these scrimmages were not a big boost for team morale.

The last game of the 1901 season pitted Notre Dame against the professional South Bend Studebakers. Both McWeeney and O'Dea played for the Studebakers and despite their struggles to dominate Notre Dame football, both dropped the college team like a bad habit a week before the

game. The Irish, left in the hands of signal-calling Red Salmon, were hardly expected to make a game of it.

Fact is, Red Salmon was more than a match for both of his coaches. While preparing for the contest, Salmon paged through his football rules book and found several outdated kicking statutes that had been ignored for years. Armed with these, Salmon devised a series of weird and complicated plays that drove the Studebakers crazy.

The game was more of a set-up than an upset. Notre Dame kicked the ball forward instead of hiking it back. They brought the ball in bounds by touching it to the sidelines and kicking it upfield. If this sounds confusing to you, pity the poor Studebakers. Back then these kicking plays were all legal, but Notre Dame's opponents had never seen the like. McWeeney and O'Dea, who had gleefully anticipated pinning back the college boys' ears, found themselves guessing along with everyone else as to just what their abandoned students would do next. At the gun, the Studebakers were wrecked on the tail-end of a 22-6 score.

The South Bend locker room exploded. The humilitated Studebakers blamed McWeeney and O'Dea for the loss. The Notre Dame coaches blamed each other, and a brawl ensued. Not just towel snapping — these guys were throwing punches.

This incident, in turn, cast a dark shadow over the Golden Dome. Father Morrissey, the University President, fired both coaches and called Red Salmon into his office. "Do you need a coach?" asked Morrissey. "Don't you know the game yourselves?" Like all great leaders, Morrissey had a knack of phrasing questions so that you knew they were orders. Salmon got the message: no more football coaches at Notre Dame. Father Morrissey suggested the team be run somewhat along the lines of an interhall squad.

In 1902, the Blue and Gold were 5-2-1, not bad for a headless body. By 1903, Notre Dame was an astounding 8-0-1; incredibly, not a point was scored against them. Few football teams in history have been able to shut out all their opponents. Notre Dame has never done it again. In 1903, they did it without a coach.

What if this defensive miracle were to occur today? The head coach, hailed nationwide as a genius, would graciously thank his two defensive coordinators, who would thank the three spotters in the press box, who would thank the four fellows who make up the scouting reporters, who would thank the five guys who take the movies, who would thank on and on and on . . .

Just how important are coaches, anyway?

* * *

If you peruse your official *Notre Dame Football Guide* you will notice one J. F. Farragher listed as the head coach for the years of 1902 and 1903. He wasn't given that title until the 1930's, and then at the whim of an unknown athletic department staffer. Farragher is Notre Dame's phantom coach.

A stout lineman for the Domers in 1900 and 1901, Farragher lent Red Salmon a hand with the 1902 squad, then returned to his home state of Ohio to go into business. He remained there until the mid-thirties, when he returned to Notre Dame and took a job as a campus cop.

A couple of years after Farragher's return, the athletic office began compiling an official record of the men who had played and coached for the Irish. Old pictures, programs, and game accounts were scrutinized, and the list swelled to near completion. But there was a conspicuous bare spot: no coach in

1902 and 1903. Someone remembered that Jim Farragher, the likable, one-eyed security guard, had helped with the team way-back-when. That was good enough for the athletic department. The man's name was inked into the blanks.

So in one swoop of the pen J. F. Farragher attained a status men dream of: Head Coach at Notre Dame.

He didn't even have to interview for the job.

* * *

Farragher.

"As usual, Salmon was the star." Almost *every* account of Notre Dame's 1902 and 1903 campaigns contains that sentence. Salmon is largely forgotten now. He made the mistake of playing in an age when newspapers did not devote pae after page to sporting news, when football games and church socials drew about the same number of people. The few who can remember seeing him in action, however, rank him as one of the finest if not the best of all Notre Dame fullbacks.

The alabaster-skinned Salmon has been described as both a slasher and a smasher, a colorful way of saying he would run right over you if he could not run around you. Salmon kicked off, punted, and drop-kicked field goals and extra points with deadly accuracy. He returned kicks, blocked exceptionally well, and — in those days of one-platoon football — was Notre Dame's outstanding linebacker. Had the forward pass been legal, he would undoubtedly have mastered it as well.

The 1902 and 1903 squads had no head coach, but they had Captain Salmon. He provided more than enough leadership for the Irish to post a solid two year record of 15-3-1, including that awesome unscored-upon season of 1903. Ironically, after Salmon actually became the coach in 1904, Notre Dame finished a lackluster 5-4. The team needed Salmon on the field, not the sidelines.

As soon as he received his engineering degree, Salmon left Notre Dame. He returned to campus only twice. The University's most popular football star disliked the idea of people making a full over him.

Best of all, this pigskin magician never marred his football career with a personal agent, contractual agent, press agent or theatrical agent. He had no private lawyer, accountant, **secretary**, valet, answering service or mail drop. No one offered Red Salmon big money to brush, spray, comb, shave, or scrub with various cosmetics. Nor did he model panty hose, lip balm, or department store leisure suits. He never worried about the Heisman trophy, the pro draft, bowl games, or the NCAA, because they did not exist.

Red Salmon played the game because it was fun. This makes him our hero forever.

★ ★ ★

★ ★ ★

Until 1912, the football was described in the rule book simply as a "prolate spheroid twenty-seven inches in circumference." A pretty vague description, especially if you don't know what prolate means. (It means the opposite of oblate.) Numerous balls can squeeze into that wide category, and most of them were used at one time or another during footballs formative years. More than one argument began simply because the visiting team couldn't recognize the shape of the ball they had been handed for the kickoff.

The turn-of-the-century pigskin had two other major faults. Because it was sewn without a lining, it frequently lost its contour and evolved into a misshapen melon as the game wore on. Besides this, the old prolate spheroid had an affinity for water and mud, greedily soaking up as much as possible, perhaps in memory of happy days in the pigpen. After the 1902 Notre Dame-Purdue tussle, the wet, muddy, lopsided ball weighed in at fourteen pounds. Fourteen pounds! Still, Red Salmon averaged thirty yards with his punts.

Ace bandage, Red?

★ ★ ★

The modern football player, you are always told, is not only bigger and stronger. He's faster. You should have been around for the second half of the 1902 American Medical game.

When George Nyere skedaddled 106 yards for a touchdown, timekeeper Pete Crumley lunged excitedly onto the field. "He's just broken the world's record for the hundred yard dash!" shouted Crumley.

The referee tried to shoo the timekeeper back to the sidelines. Crumley would not be moved. He was flabbergasted. He kept insisting something important had happened.

According to the *Notre Dame Scholastic,* it took the official and about forty bystanders almost five minutes "to convince Pete that the contest was a football game and not a track meet." The game continued, a 92-0 romp for the Irish.

Nyere's time, whatever it was, was not recorded.

★ ★ ★

Louis Wagner won renown for kicking Hershbergers. Not that Wagner was carrying on some weird vendetta against the family Hershberger. Quite the contrary.

Before the advent of the forward pass, the only spirals on a football field were the rare accidental ones flying off a punter's foot. In this era when kicking was so vitally important, punters booted end-over-end jobs, fluttering ducks, wobbling gliders, anything to get their teams in better position. To most punters, spirals were as essential as napkin rings at the training table. They might bring an "ooohh" from the crowd; other than that, what good were they?

Then a Chicago kid named Hershberger developed a novel way of punting that produced a spiral every time. On receiving the pass from center, Hershberger lifted the ball over his head, and slammed the pigskin onto the foot that was sweeping up to kick the ball. *Viola!* The punt whorled majestically downfield with uncanny accuracy and distance. A spiral was no longer called a spiral. It was called a Hershberger.

And that brings us back to Louis Wagner. He was one of the few Notre Damers who mastered the now lost and forgotten art of booting a Hershberger.

Think you're coordinated? Give it a try.

★ ★ ★

The uniforms of the day, as you can see by the photographs in this chapter, fall somewhat below today's standards.

Helmets appeared in the Gay Nineties, but most players preferred to butt heads without them. Simple cloth caps and even bare heads were the height of style for several seasons.

After its initial appearance in 1890, the noseguard enjoyed about fifteen years of popularity. A bulky, canvas-covered frame that strapped to the middle of the face, this device gave the most fearsome footballer the look of an exotic bird. The main drawback of the noseguard was its pronounced tendency to suffocate the user; this resulted in its eventual abandonment.

Shoulder and elbow pads were sometimes sewn into the unnumbered jerseys, offering peace of mind but no real protection, like an insurance policy with unwittingly lapsed premiums. In addition, the early Notre Dame hero could wear a canvas smock or vest that usually attached to the pants.

Ah, the pants. The football trousers weighed nearly as much as one of today's compact cars, and were just as confining. Thick were these pants, stuffed with paper mache and splints and other padding that made for pretty slow going, especially in wet weather. The pants acted as a sponge.

Shin guards were fairly widespread around the turn of the century, but were dropped by teams looking for a lighter, faster attack.

Shoes were heavy, sacrificing speed for protection. Cleats caught hold in 1890, but many players considered them more of a nuisance than anything else.

Footballers did not tape up before a game. They waited until afterwards when, because of their equipment, they needed not only tape but sterile gauze and a few cold compresses.

★ ★ ★

The all time record for yards gained by a Notre Dame offense was set October 24, 1908 against the Chicago Physicians and Surgeons: 1,306 yards, approximately three quarters of a mile.

★ ★ ★

Our old high school coach was wont to trill:

Do you have big D?
My, oh yes . . .
Big D, little e-s-i-r-e
Yes!

. . . or something like that.

While this clearly explains why the old boy is now hawking life insurance, it also brings up the subject of Desire, which is something football coaches rate miles ahead of breathing. "Desire" is a catch-all for drive, determination, dedication, all those forceful

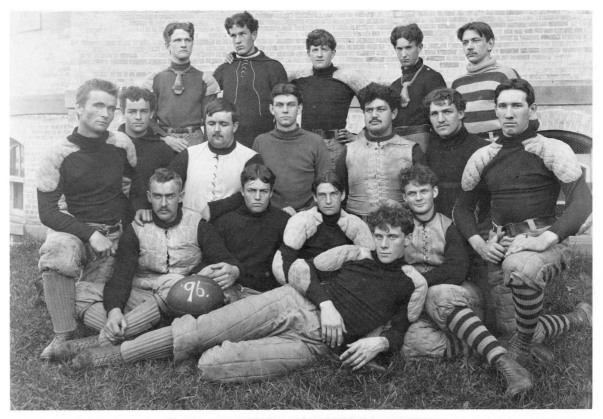

A nice smattering of primitive equipment here: nose guards, shin guards, sewn-in padding, and a melon-shaped ball.

sounding "D" words that a coach would fling at you when he saw you lagging a bit on the push-ups. Some players, the coach would declare, succeed on desire alone. Some on talent. And some — here you could see the mentor's mouth watering slightly — have them both.

For all you coaches out there, may we present Red Miller? He had them both, in great abundance.

A four year letterman, Miller was blessed with lightning speed, uncanny instincts, and an unnatural love of practice. He almost ruined his legs and did wear out several pairs of shoes teaching himself to stop "dead" from full speed in two steps. When no one else would practice with him, Miller set up staggered track hurdles. Hour after hour he would weave his way through these make-believe tacklers, learning to juke, sidestep, shift gears. In later seasons, he practiced with his coach's Boston bull pup. The Irish star and the little dog dodged and chased each other all over the field; the pup always tuckered out first.

Miller played thirty-one games with his self-taught swift and swerving style honed to perfection. The Notre Dame halfback barely had time to strike up a passing acquaintance with the opposition. He was always off on another long run.

As if his own accomplishments were not enough, Miller blazed the trail for the rest of the family. To date, the Defiance, Ohio, Millers have sent more great football players to Notre Dame than most Western states.

Say, coaches, let's hear it for Harry (Red) Miller:

> *Did he have Big D?*
> *My, oh yes . . .*

* * *

Part of the Miller dynasty: (from left) Don (class of 1925); Gerry (1925); Walter (1920); Ray (1913); and Harry (1910).

LEGEND: In the 1909 Michigan game, Pete Vaughan scored from five yards out, exploding through the line with such force that he broke the goalpost with his head.

FACT: Vaughn wasn't sure if it was his head or his shoulder that snapped the goalpost. "I didn't feel a thing," he insisted.

(There are smart people today who think this is why helmets were invented — to protect goalposts.)

★ ★ ★

He had the best won-lost percentage of any Notre Dame football coach. You've never heard of him.

In two years, his teams outscored their opponents 611 to 36 points. You've still never heard of him.

He was Notre Dame's only undefeated coach. Stop guessing.

He was John L. Marks.

(Who?)

Coaching in 1911 and 1912, Marks was largely responsible for introducing modern football to Notre Dame. He shaped the Gold and Blue from a plunge, a punt and a prayer into a swift and slashing scoring machine. Suddenly, Notre Dame was not just outplaying their opponents — they were out-thinking them. That's the way the Irish have been winning ever since.

It was Marks, in fact, who created the passing combination of Gus Dorais to Knute Rockne. It was Marks who first tapped the line busting power of Fullback Ray Eichenlaub. When Coach Jesse Harper's team destroyed Army in 1913, it did so with an offense mostly of Marks' invention.

John L. Marks, however, isn't given much credit

Shy, sensitive Pete Vaughan, who snapped goalposts with his head and looks like he could eat cactus for breakfast.

Ray Eichenlaub, also known as Iron Eich, The Two-Hundred Pound Torpedo.

for any of this. His legacy has all but disappeared.

The next time you toast the Irish, would you lift a glass to John L. Marks?

★   ★   ★

He was a modern football coach all right. Sure proof of this is the delight John L. Marks felt in running it up and piling it on. The 69-0 embarrassment of Marquette, the 80-0 route of Loyola, the 116-7 dismemberment of St. Viator — Marks lapped them all like an early version of a big-time coach trying to hype his team's ratings.

In a 1912 game with Adrian, Notre Dame had built up a small cushion of 61-0 when the hapless Adrian coach trotted over to Marks.

"I'm out of players." The Bulldog coach swept a paw toward his tattered squad. "Used up all my substitutes."

Under the era's strict no-substitution rules, this called for a forfeit. John L. Marks, however, was not about to stop a game that was so much fun. Magnanimously, he waived the rule on substitutes. "Send in men who have already played," he cheerfully insisted, and the contest continued.

Late in the game, which had become a slaughter somewhat approximating the Massacre of the Innocents, Marks spotted a strange face on the Notre Dame sidelines. It was an Adrian player.

"You're on the wrong bench," barked Marks.

"I know," whined the battered Bulldog. "I've been in there four times already. They're not sending me back if I can help it."

Merciless he was not. Marks let the kid hide.

★   ★   ★

An Irishman, recently arrived from the *auld sod*, was hearing about American football for the first time. Try as he might, he could not quite grasp the finer points of the game. Finally he interrupted his instructor.

"Let me see if I understand," mused the Hibernian. "The game goes like this: the ball is hiked and the fight begins."

Well, he was told, that's basically true.

"I'd love to play."

But we have no ball.

"To hell with the ball," stormed the Celt. "Let's start the game."

★

No one knows exactly how Notre Dame's Fighting Irish got their name. Admittedly, four Irish brothers did aid Founding Father Sorin in establishing the University. The French-born Sorin, however, was never very fond of Celts. "Not inclined to obedience," was his comment on the Irish.

When a 1904 *Milwaukee Sentinel* noted the school's line-up of "Fighting Irishmen," nobody noticed. Early newspapers commonly referred to the football team as the Notre Dames or Notre Damers, the Gold and Blue, Warriors, Domers, Benders and South Benders, Hoosiers, and Catholics. Playing without a home stadium for over forty years, Notre Dame was nicknamed the Nomads and Ramblers. (One sportswriter called them the Road Scholars.) Rockne's teams, especially fast and flashy for their era, were tabbed the Rockets and Blue Comets.

★

NOTRE DAME

Father Sorin's statue after a recent St. Patrick's Day — **he's still having trouble with the Irish.**

During the 1909 Michigan game, hard-headed Pete Vaughan is reputed to have blasted his teammates: "What's the matter with you guys? You're all Irish and you're not fighting!" Well, you can't insult an Irishman any worse than that, except by refusing to drink with him. Incensed, Notre Dame thumped the Wolverines 11-3. It may have seemed like a mandate, but the Fighting Irish nickname faded quickly in the glow of victory.

Notre Dame Alumnus Francis Wallace probably deserves most of the credit (or blame, however you want to look at it) for the Fighting Irish label. Wallace started using the term in the 1920's in his *New York Daily News* football columns. The name fit; and after a while the name stuck. America had seen enough Celtic immigrants to know that Fighting and Irish go together like tick and tock.

Most Notre Dame administrators disliked the Fighting Irish tag. For years they tried to play it down, forget about it, pretend it did not exist. Of course, they did the same thing with women. The University is stuck with them now, too.

★ ★ ★

Whatever the team was called, the school always had its share of Fighting Irish. Take the glorious example of Pete Dwyer in the 1909 Pitt game. Pete was the Notre Dame quarterback, and very good at noticing things. In this game for instance, Pete noted that his squad was being penalized on almost every offensive play. This did not sit well with him. After one long walk-off, Pete did some arithmetic in his head and discovered that Notre Dame had forfeited more yardage against Pitt than in all previous games combined. A small, nasty thought flitted across his brain. "We're being cheated," Pete told himself.

This was an injustice, and the last Irishman to quietly suffer an injustice was bound and gagged and locked in a soundproof room. Pete fussed. He fretted. He was just about to launch a major protest when he was ordered off the field.

Did our man waltz submissively to the sidelines? With Principle at stake? Are you kidding? This break in the action gave Pete the very opportunity he wanted, which was to punch, er, have a little chat with the referee.

Here, the official commited his only really unforgivable error of the afternoon: he chose not to run. The two met near midfield. Pete made it a point to double his fists before talking. The official decided to hide behind his office, which makes a very poor shield. "I'm going to smack you in the mouth," said Pete. And he did.

"No penalty!" cried Pete's teammates. "No penalty!" There was no rule in the book about a referee getting his lights punched out. Besides, the blow was struck by an ineligible player.

Good thinking, Irish!

Notre Dame was penalized forty-five yards.

★ ★ ★

By the 1913 Army game, the Irish were wiser. Fitz Fitzgerald, slyer than Dwyer, decided to make the referee call one for Notre Dame, like it or not.

Fitz waited until the official was otherwise occupied. He then walked over to the Army center, Johnny McEwen, and gave him a pop in the nose. "Hey, ref!" yelled Fitz. The official turned just in time to see McEwen's retaliation, a right to Fitzgerald's jaw.

No penalty.

★ ★ ★

To give them their due, referees were often poorly trained and paid in football's emerging years. Usually local talent, the officials were understandably sympathetic to the home team when the press boxes were as partisan as the crowds, and the peering eyes of television and the NCAA had not yet blinked open.

The well-travelled Fighting Irish were often victims of wildly fluctuating rules interpretations. What was plainly illegal in one conference was honest, hard-nosed football in the next. Then there was the occasional official who — much as he tried to maintain a veneer of neutrality — was nothing less than the other team's twelfth man.

One such referee was giving the visiting Irish a tough time during a tight contest. The ball was fumbled. A knot of players from both sides chased it, slapped it, kicked it, and finally succeeded in batting the pigskin out of bounds.

"Our ball!" cried a man from Notre Dame.

"Oh, no," answered the official. "*Our* ball."

★ ★ ★

Shorty Longman probably knew it was a mistake when Bob Matthews slipped his first punch. Here was Longman, Notre Dame's coach, in the ring with one of his own players. The whole idea was to teach the team the importance of the pugilistic arts. Besides that, Longman wanted them all to know he could swat them down like flies if need be. It helped discipline.

Longman had picked a lightweight for the first boxing lesson. Bob Matthews was as thin as six o'clock, a mild-mannered, bewildered looking end that Longman figured to have on the canvas inside of a minute.

Matthews, however, had forgotten more about boxing than Longman would ever know. The player ducked his coach's initial haymakers. Then he went on the attack. Expertly hooking, jabbing, and flat-out punching, Matthews fought with the blithe abandon of anyone just given permission to bop the boss in the nose.

A little learning is indeed a dangerous thing. At the end of his round with Matthews, Longman wobbled to the ropes and imparted his newfound wisdom to the team:

"No more boxing lessons!"

* * *

Shorty Longman looked ridiculous in the ring. He had no intention of letting his team look foolish on the field.

The modern spiral pass really irritated the Notre Dame coach. "Spirals won't work on a rainy day," Longman told his quarterbacks. "You can't grip a wet football. Your passes will fall flat as a rock."

Longman decided to use Gus Dorais, a pint-sized freshman from Wisconsin, in a little demonstration. After soaking a football in water for over an hour, Longman handed the dripping pigskin to Dorais. The Wisconsin kid flipped a long, accurate spiral. Dorais got the wet ball back and tossed another long bomb. And another. And another, until Longman walked away, muttering to himself.

One thing you can say about Shorty Longman. He was no teacher, but he certainly learned well. Dorais was the regular quarterback within three weeks.

* * *

The best thing Shorty Longman did for Notre Dame was resign. If Longman had not quit, one of his freshman footballers was going to.

The name of that flagging frosh was Knute Rockne. The implications are staggering, aren't they?

* * *

"Hazing," a word that has faded completely from the campus vocabulary, played an important role in Notre Dame's formative years. The term refers to an initiation given to students whose behavior was considered nonconformist. For instance, the slackards who didn't get out of bed to greet a returning football team at the train station were subject to a dunking in the icy waters of St. Mary's Lake. That was a lesson quickly learned.

The prescribed forms of hazing became tradition, and were handed from class to class like treasured heirlooms. "Steam rent" was a sum of money collected from freshmen early in their first semester. Seniors wielding monkey wrenches would go from room to room threatening to disconnect radiators if prompt payment was not made.

There was the "Black Cat Club." Prospective members were blindfolded. They were given two black cats to hold by the tails, one in each hand — no small chore in itself, since cats never see the humor in that arrangement. Finally, trailed by a group of people red-faced with suppressed laughter, the initiate was ushered across campus at midnight and told to knock on the "clubhouse door." Surprise! The door belonged to the Prefect of Discipline.

The most elaborate hazing ever hatched was the crowning of the Notre Dame Marbles Champion. Rupe Mills, Ray Eichenlaub, and Knute Rockne were three who helped conceive and direct the scheme.

In the spring of 1913, a bespectacled freshman named Glen Herricks made it known to all of Brownson Hall that he was the marbles champ in his hometown, and that he was willing to take on all comers in his sport. Braggadocio was a no-no for a first-year man. Young Mr. Herricks had just bought himself a one-way ticket on the Initiation Express.

Not long after he had claimed his prowess at marbles Eichenlaub, Mills, and several others escorted him to the fieldhouse, where Knute Rockne was rolling billiard balls into a huge circle drawn on the floor. "What does he think he's doing?" asked Herricks.

"These are college marbles, Glen," explained Eichenlaub. "That's an intercollegiate marbles ring. And Rock here is the campus champion."

Rockne glanced up from the floor, acknowledging their presence for the first time. "I hear you're pretty good," he said to Herricks. "I don't get much competition around here. How about a match?"

Herricks accepted. Despite his unfamiliarity with the college marbles he bested Rockne, beat Eichenlaub and Mills, and in the following days continued undefeated against all contenders. Soon he was leading the sweet life of a champion: a trainer bandaged his shooting hand every morning before classes; a promoter made sure all title matches had adequate publicity. Eventually the entire student body became aware of the scam, and would give the champ a standing ovation when he entered the dining hall.

Seeking to end the poor youngster's delusions, Father Matt Walsh summoned Herricks to his office. "Glen," he cautioned, "the students are putting you on. There's no such thing as the marbles champion. Now don't get into any more of those games that they want you to play."

Armed with this information Herricks confronted his tormentors. They laughed. Father Walsh, they told him, was a past marbles champion who wanted the crown for himself; but his skills were in their twilight years and he had to resort to trickery. "He says the same thing to every new champ," someone remarked.

So the charade continued. Then, ominous

rumors swept the campus. It was whispered that Glen Herricks was a professional! Witnesses came forward, declaring that they had seen the champ hustling Lake Michigan tourists at marbles during the summer. Herricks anxiously denied the charges. But because of the dimensions of the scandal a trial became necessary.

The champ in custody.

Glen Herricks' championship form.

A title defense.

A full-scale kangaroo court, with a judge, a jury, and staffs for the prosecution and defense, convened one spring evening on the first floor of Washington Hall. The accused, plainly scared out of his wits, was led in through a crowd of hissing spectators.

One of the spectators had a special interest. He was Father Burke, the Prefect of Discipline. Crouched surreptitiously outside a window, he watched the proceedings — with a fire hose in his hands. As the court was called to order he eased open the window and signalled an acolyte to turn on the water full-blast. The jet from the hose caught the students off guard. Panic-stricken, they scrambled to get out the door, like rats seeking darkness. Father Burke had accomplished his mission.

The crown of Notre Dame Marbles Champion was finally laid to rest. It took a death-by-drowning to do it.

★ ★ ★

So many marvelous things have been written about the 1913 Notre Dame-Army game, it's a shame not more of them are true.

Coach Jesse Harper supposedly initiated the action by boldly writing a letter to West Point requesting a game. In fact, Harper only answered a letter from Cadet Football Manager, Harold Loomis.

Loomis was in a pickle. The Yale game had been cancelled for fear it would "take too much out of the boys." It was a little late in the year to start wiping teams off the slate. Anxious to plug the schedule, Loomis wrote to virtually every school that crossed his mind. Thanks to the machinations of three guys named Rockne, Dorais, and Bill Cotter, the Irish had just been signed to play baseball. Would they try football as well? Happily, Notre Dame had an open date on November 1, and the game was on.

After some initial grumbling, Army coughed up the $1,000 guarantee Harper demanded. (These same Army guys, who balked at spending $1,000, later went to the Pentagon and could ask Congress for a billion without batting an eyelid.) The point was, Eastern teams usually paid their own way. But impoverished Notre Dame was in no position to put on airs. To save money, the boys packed their own lunches and boarded a railroad day coach to the East. Every player carried his own equipment, not an easy task since most did not own a suitcase. Did we say impoverished? Some of the Irish were wearing football shoes sans cleats. It was the best they could do.

★

You have probably read somewhere that Army expected the Notre Dame players to take the field barefoot, shouldering cane fishing poles, and wearing straw hats, wondering what this new-fangled football was all about. Actually, Notre Dame's reputation as a Midwest powerhouse had preceded them. The Cadets expected nothing but hard-hitting, though most thought it would be only a very tough warm-up for the annual battle with Navy.

As you know, the game turned out to be the biggest Army disaster since the Battle of Bull Run. Thumbing their noses at prevailing football strategy, the Notre Damers pulled stunts like winning the toss and choosing to receive the kick-off; or using all four downs before punting. Most of all, the visitors displayed a stunningly effective use of the forward pass. By game's end, Notre Dame had swallowed up the Cadets, 35-15.

★

Did the game mark (as some have claimed) the invention of the forward pass? Of course not. Was forward passing still so rare that the West Pointers were dumbfounded to actually see an airborne swineskin? Hardly. In fact, Army was one of the premiere passing teams of the East. The Cadets tossed several aerials in the Notre Dame game, one of which was intercepted in the end zone by Irish quarterback Gus Dorais.

Army's problems were philosophical. Cadet Coach Charly Daly, as almost everyone else, considered the pass a dangerous weapon of the last resort, sort of a football Doomsday Machine. Passes were to be thrown only in the opponent's territory, only as the half neared a close, only when all other means of attack had failed. When Army did pass, the attempt was laughably stodgy. Cadet quarterbacks tossed "spot" passes: an Army receiver would run to a spot and wait, thumbs twiddling, for the ball to arrive.

Notre Dame's aerial warfare was as modern as today's. Gus Dorais led his receivers with the ball so that the Irish could catch the pigskin on the dead run. To an Army player, used to turning and standing and waiting for a flat pass to hit him in the chest, it must have seemed as though the Notre Damers were plucking footballs out of midair. Dorais launched passes of thirty-five and forty yards — incredible distances in those days — that had the partisan Army crowd wowing and cheering in spite of itself.

Most importantly, Notre Dame used the pass in conjunction with the run, in an integrated offense that every football team (even those from the Big Ten) uses to this day. No longer was the forward pass merely a losing coach's anxiety attack. Dorais used runs to set up passes, and passes to set up runs, and played the Army defense like a slide trombone. When the Cadets closed in to cover an

Eichenlaub line plunge, Dorais flipped to Rockne or Pliska. When Army scattered to defense the pass, Irish runners smashed up the middle. This is the only kind of football we have ever seen, but it was all news to Army that day, and it drove them to a dizzying defeat.

The question remains: Did Notre Dame keep their blitzkrieg under wraps until the West Point game? Absolutely not. Army had scouts in South Bend, and should have known the Irish attack weeks in advance. Still, as Army glumly admitted after the defeat, they had no idea what hit them. Makes you want to build a bomb shelter, doesn't it?

★

How important was this game? Well, it was as if a new base had been added in baseball, or a couple of extra goals in hockey. Until this time, football had been won with kicking, brute strength, and defense. All at once, the compass swung toward offense, where it has remained ever since.

Actually, so many Eastern football experts accused the Cadets of dogging it against Notre Dame that the real test of open football came in that year's Army-Navy game. West Point proved its own defeat was no fluke by adopting the Notre Dame attack to sink a superior Midshipmen squad, 22-9. So much for experts.

It would be nice to say, as most believe, that the Notre Dame-Army game established the superiority of Midwestern football. Unfortunately, the Irish traveled to Yale a year later and were mauled, 28-0. Nor was the Army game the victory of a young upstart over an old, established football power. The Cadets had started playing football in 1890, three years after Notre Dame. By 1913, both were regional powerhouses. The 35-13 Irish win was not as amazing an upset as the Eastern provincials claimed.

For Notre Dame, the Army game was a chance to jump into big-time nationwide football. The Irish victory, and the startling manner of it, won them a place forever. Notre Dame got some badly-needed recognition, which translated into dollars. Schools were suddenly anxious to schedule the Irish, fans were willing to pay for a glimpse of their new style of play. The football team was about to become the University's number one fund-raiser; Notre Dame has remained "that football school" ever since.

★ ★ ★

By the way, the one story you always hear about this game is true. After Army's defeat, an officer was seen near the sidelines, snarling at his wife:

"Well, you've been hollering about why don't we play some decent opposition. Now, dammit, are you satisfied?"

★ ★ ★

The victory over Army was easily the high point of that undefeated 1913 season. The following week's game against Penn State was very nearly a disaster.

No sooner did the travel-weary team return from New York than it boarded a Thursday train for Northern Pennsylvania and a meeting with the Nittnay Lions. To stay within his shoestring budget, Harper wired State's coach and arranged for Notre Dame to stay in a campus dorm the night before the game. The coach was only too happy to oblige. After reading of of the thrashing that Notre Dame gave Army he was sure his team was overmatched. Now, he would have the enemy in his camp. He set about concocting the old equalizer.

That Friday night Notre Dame's entire nineteen-man traveling squad found itself lodged in a

cramped, drafty dormitory room. They were served an evening meal that detonated in their stomachs like a depth charge. "We got physicked," recalls a reserve tackle, implying that their fish contained a Mickey Finn. No one on the team got much sleep; they were too busy feeling ill.

The next day Notre Dame took the field looking as if they'd spent a winter at Valley Forge. To compound their miseries, the game was played in a chilling drizzle. The attack that had been so crisp against Army faltered badly as the pale, dispirited Ramblers could not get untracked. The game was an artistic flop. "We ran for a lot of yardage that day," says the reserve, "most of it back and forth to the bathroom." Only Dorais' consistent punting kept the South Benders out of a hole, and allowed them to escape with a 14-7 victory.

Until its loss to Notre Dame, Penn State had never been beaten on its home field, an undefeated skein that stretched back nineteen years. Wonder why?

★ ★ ★

When Rockne's mother arrived from Chicago to see her first game, the Rock found her a choice seat and put on a memorable show. Thanks to the sympathetic play-calling of Gus Dorais, Rock caught more than his share of passes, was able to throw some highly-conspicuous blocks, and scored more points than ever before. Afterwards, the Notre Dame end proudly asked his mom what she thought of the game.

"Wonderful!" said Mrs. Rockne. "I particularly like that fellow who did the pinwheels. I could hardly take my eyes off him."

"Mother, that was the cheerleader!"

★ ★ ★

★   ★   ★

Thomas Edison said it: Genius is 1% inspiration, 99% perspiration. He should have also squeezed out a percentage point for luck.

During the 1913 Penn State contest, Knute Rockne was scooting out for a pass when he slipped and fell. The pursuing State back overran him. Rockne scrambled to his feet and was in the clear for the quick pass flipped to him by Dorais.

This lucky mistake worked so well that our heroes decided to build a play around it. They called it the button-hook pass. Today the button-hook is so basic, so common, we forget someone had to invent it.

Rockne was two steps ahead of everyone even when he was falling down on the job.

★   ★   ★

Alfred Morales, the self-proclaimed King of the Mexicans, attempted a flying tackle along the sidelines in a 1916 game. He missed the runner, but hit a parked car and broke his collarbone.

★   ★   ★

II.
Notre Dame's All-Time Opponents

Conjures up visions of Southern Cal, Purdue, Pitt and Army doesn't it? Ah,
but there are a few we've forgotten. The following list is authentic. So are the scores.

ND 62   CHICAGO DENTAL 0
You can just see these guys about to run a play, staring into the Notre Dame line and cooing, "Now, open wide."

ND 32   ALMA 0
Later merged with Mater.

ND 34   MICHIGAN AGRICULTURAL 6
Produced several All-America groundskeepers.

ND 46   SOUTH BEND ATHLETIC CLUB 0
Obviously as athletic as most athletic clubs.

ND 20   HARVARD SCHOOL OF CHICAGO 0
A branch of that place out East, no doubt.

ND 18   ILLINOIS CYCLING CLUB 2
Ever try to tackle a guy on a unicycle?

ND 5   KNOX 12
You've heard of its sister institution, the school of hard Knox.

ND 39   MORRIS HARVEY 0
The famous one-man team.

ND 60   ROSE POLY 11
Thank heavens we won this one. I mean, how embarrassing to lose to a team named Rose Poly! How tough could they possibly be? And what color do you suppose their uniforms were?

ND 0   INDIANAPOLIS ARTILLERY 18
Talk about being on the front lines. Those guys in the Indy Artillery never knew when they could be called up to fight off an invasion from Kokomo.

ND 14   IOWA PRE-FLIGHT 13
Couldn't quite get off the ground.

ND 20   CHRISTIAN BROTHERS 7
Fratricide.

ND 14   KALAMAZOO 0
Except for its series of seven games with Notre Dame, and the fact that Tex Beneke had a gal there, there's not much you can say about Kalamazoo.

ND 55   RICE 2
You've heard of minute rice? That's how long these guys were in the game.

ND 20   NORTHWESTERN LAW 0
Led the league in arguments.

ND 28   COE 7
The famous Coe champions.

ND —   TRANSYLVANIA —
Cancelled. Too many of the Notre Dame players insisted on wearing crucifixes.

ND 6   TOLEDO A.A. 0
Double-check those water bottles.

ND 56   SOUTH BEND HIGH 0

ND 29   ENGLEWOOD HIGH 5

ND 44   NORTH DIVISION HIGH 0
This had to make recruiting easier. If any of these high schoolers gave the Irish particular trouble, they could enroll him in Notre Dame before the next game.

ND 32   **CHICAGO PHYSICIANS AND SURGEONS 0**

ND 18   **RUSH MEDICAL 6**

ND 6   **OHIO MEDICAL 0**

ND 22   **BENNETT MEDICAL 0**

ND 28   **MISSOURI OSTEOPATHIC 0**
Of course, the above scores are from the days when doctors actually played something else besides golf.

Why don't medical schools have football teams any more? Perhaps the answer lies in American Medical's series with Notre Dame:

1902
ND 92   **AMERICAN MEDICAL 0**
Hmm, some slight room for improvement on Am Med's part.

1903
ND 52   **AMERICAN MEDICAL 0**
What a job! In one year they've amputated forty points from Notre Dame's score. Not many teams can do that and still lose by over fifty.

1904
ND 44   **AMERICAN MEDICAL 0**
A veritable cliff-hanger. It was anybody's ball game there until the kickoff.

1905
ND 142   **AMERICAN MEDICAL 0**
End of series. Bow your heads, please. This team is showing no vital signs. Thank God these guys could double as their own trainers.

III.
Rock Around the Clock
1918-1930

To understand Knute Rockne, you must understand his age. Turn first to the newspapers. Radio and film were comparative infants; slick magazines and digests yet unborn. The daily newspaper was diversion, entertainment, information for an American public increasingly burdened with leisure time. The best writers were journalists. The finest copy was frequently found in the sports section.

A proven circulation boost, sports coverage exploded from the two or three columns of days past. Editors and writers discovered America's hunger for heroes, the glamorous, colorful kings of the sporting world. The dailies responded by creating America's first sports superstars. There was Tilden in tennis; Bobby Jones on the golf course; Dempsey in the ring; Man O'War on the racetrack; baseball's Babe Ruth. The football demi-god was Rockne. His team was Notre Dame.

Surprisingly, Rockne was everything the papers said about him: the greatest football coach of all time. His record is too well known to belabor here. His teams won 105 games, lost 12, tied 5. They were named Western Champions in 1919 and 1920, National Champs in 1924, 1929 and 1930. Including ties, Rockne's teams lost but one game in twenty.

Statistics so faintly echo this man of superlatives. He was a character builder in an age when people still believed in that sort of work. Rockne set a standard of excellence which brought unprecedented fame, wealth and the allegiance of millions to his school. For the public, Rockne was football; football was Rockne. More than any other man, he planted a love of the game in the American psyche.

Three weeks before Rockne finished his first year (1918) as head coach at Notre Dame with an unpromising 3-1-2 record, the Great War in Europe had ground to a halt. America roared into the Twenties, discovering bathing beauty contests, Bolsheviks, B.O., bobbed hair, and *Babbit*. Prohibition fermented into speakeasies and bootlegging. Ninety miles up the road from Notre Dame, Scarface Al Capone made millions by giving a guy a place to buy a drink.

Women started wearing make-up, still calling it "paint." Sheiks met flaming mamies on the dance floor where everybody was doing the Charleston. When Al Jolson stood up in *The Jazz Singer* and belted out a song that the audience could hear, it was the world's first talking movie.

Hemingway and Faulkner tried to make sense out of it all. Goat-nosed Henry Luce got *Time* running; Herbert Ross started the *New Yorker*. Two fellows named Simon and Schuster released a book of crossword puzzles that created a national craze.

Odd looking devices, traffic lights, sprang up everywhere. Lindbergh beat the Atlantic. The Bible won out in the Scopes-monkey trial. Newspaper sensationalism scraped a new low in the "Pig Woman" murder case. The great Florida land boom was followed swiftly by the great Florida land bust.

Then the 1929 stock market crash ended it all. But we are getting far ahead of ourselves. Let's reel back to the beginning of the age of Rockne.

★　★　★

Notre Dame made its name by scheduling — and beating — bigger and more famous opponents. Scheduling the games was often tougher than playing them.

Remember, football wars weren't plotted eight and ten years in advance as they are today. A coach usually started hunting next fall's opponents in February, and was fortunate to have a full slate by springtime.

Even as Notre Dame was becoming a nationally-popular attraction, a lot of the larger schools were out to lunch when Rockne came calling for a contest.

Bob Zuppke of Illinois, for instance, treated Notre Dame's advances like an offer to trade head shots with Jack Dempsey.

Rockne once approached the Illini coach: "How about a game this year?"

"Nothing doing," snapped Zuppke.

"We'll travel." Rockne was conciliatory. "Play you at Illinois."

"Nope."

"Listen," Rockne confided, "you could beat us easily. I lose my whole first team through graduation."

Again Zuppke demurred.

Rockne pleaded. Finally he allowed as how his whole second team would also graduate.

"In that case," grinned Zuppke. "I definitely can't schedule you. I doubt that your third team could draw much of a crowd at Illinois."

★　★　★

Every great player has a certain area of the game in which he flashes brilliance. Other quarterbacks have passed more accurately, run faster, called better plays. But Joe Brandy's teammates always remembered him for one notable achievement:

First man into the shower.

In the early years the athletic department had only one really workable shower head. The others just dripped or fizzled or splattered the ceiling. The good shower belonged to Joe Brandy.

After practice, like a champion, he streaked into the locker room. He slipped out of his uniform so fast he could make a disrobing Red Cross lifesaver look like a strip tease act. While everybody else was still peeling off socks, Joe was already camped under the lone straight, steamy spray.

★ ★ ★

Heartly "Hunk" Anderson, speaking to the student body at a pep rally: "I'll do the best we can."

★ ★ ★

The Gipper. Put him right up there on the pedestal reserved for our god-almighty American sports legends, where fact and fancy mingle until The Man is finally washed away and only The Hero remains, glowing like gold mined from a mountain creek. Who was The Gipper? And why are they winning all those football games on his account?

Have you known anyone so naturally talented at sports that he felt obliged to participate, even though he wasn't motivated by traditional values of the game? That was Gipp.

Have you known anyone who loved to bet large sums of money, especially on himself? That was Gipp.

Have you known anyone who could drop-kick a field goal from sixty yards, slam a baseball 360 feet, and run sixty balls in straight pool? Probably you haven't, but that too, was Gipp.

George Gipp hailed from Larium, Michigan, a mining town on Lake Superior's shore. He came to Notre Dame shortly after his twenty-first birthday. Billy Gray, a catcher for the White Sox who had played at Notre Dame, wangled a partial baseball scholarship for him. George liked baseball well enough, and the town of South Bend promised a few years of adventure — the two reaons he appeared on campus in the fall of 1916.

Prodded by Rockne, he went out for football, which soon became his first sport. Studying, however, remained his least favorite pastime. Gipp had an extremely quick mind and could have done well in the classroom, but he preferred to catch the

Hill Street trolley into South Bend to play some stud poker at the Oliver Hotel, or flush a pigeon at Hullie and Mike's Pool Hall. "Hell, that's how half the team earned their spending money," says Norman Barry Sr., now a judge in Chicago. "We'd cover Gipp's bets at Hullie and Mike's and he'd divvy up the winnings with us."

Gipp spent so much time in the dark, smoke-filled haunts of itinerant sharpies in low-brimmed hats and two-tone shoes, that for four years at Notre Dame his skin remained a pasty complexion; it seldom saw the light of day.

He usually wagered a bundle on Notre Dame's games, once betting he would outscore the entire Army team (he didn't). If he couldn't bring himself to do it for the glory of old Notre Dame, Gipp could nevertheless summon extraordinary powers when money was on the line. In the 1920 Indiana game he choreographed what Rockne later termed the greatest play he'd ever seen:

The Hoosiers were ahead 10-7 with sixty seconds in the game. Notre Dame had the ball, fourth and goal on Indiana's one-yard line. Naturally the defense's attention was riveted on Gipp — who was having trouble with his helmet. He fiddled with it, then pulled it off. When he did, the ball was snapped to Joe Brandy, who tip-toed across with the winning score. The Gipper, aware that he was a potent decoy, had arranged for the ball to be hiked when he popped his lid.

The repetitive nature of football practice irked George, so he seldom bothered to attend, at least until late in the week. When he did show, Rockne would bury him on the fourth team, where he'd stay until Saturday — when he would always get boosted into the starting line-up. Rock was no dummy.

To get his star to make up for lost practice time, the coach resorted to special tactics. The Irish

were comfortably ahead of Kalamazoo in 1917. Rockne called a referee to his side. "When Gipp makes a long run, I want you to call a penalty on us, whether we've committed one or not," he instructed.

Refs were more accomodating in those days. Gipp made runs of eighty and sixty-eight yards in the first half; both were nullified.

In the second period, the halfback grabbed a punt and cruised seventy yards untouched across Kalamazoo's goal line. "Bring it back!" called the referee. "Clipping, Notre Dame."

The Gipper had no fondness for frivolous exercise. He sauntered up to the official who'd been calling the penalties and dropped the ball at his feet. "Next time," he said, "give me one whistle to stop, and two to keep going."

★ ★ ★

Norman Barry dropped an easy pass in the 1920 Nebraska game. Said Gipp to Barry after the play: "Next time I'll put handlebars on it."

★ ★ ★

We mention Bud Slomar due to guilt by association, since Bud played baseball with George Gipp in the Flint, Michigan, industrial league. This is Slomar's only connection with the Fighting Irish, but he's just too good to pass up.

Slomar was proud of his ability to take a punch. So proud, in fact, that he once had Gipp fire a baseball at his head. Slomar, according to witnesses, did not blink as the ball caromed off his cranium. The stunt was a sure-fire crowd pleaser and soon became a ritual before each game. Slomar would stand some distance from Gipp, who would wind up and throw his best pitch at his friends's skull.

The ball was always the worse for wear.

★ ★ ★

Notre Dame's first eleven game season: 1921. If that won't win you five bucks in a bar bet, nothing will.

★ ★ ★

Harry "Horse" Mehre of Huntington, Indiana, insisted that all his friends and relatives attend the Notre Dame-Indiana game. "Rock said he's going to use me," Mehre promised.

In the locker room before the game, Mehre strained to hear his name in the starting line-up. Rockne read eleven names before mentioning the eager Hoosier.

"Mehre," said Rock, "will take the chains and work with the head linesman."

★ ★ ★

Some of the team's longest afternoons were spent in Lincoln, Nebraska. Not that a weekend in Lincoln is any carnival today, mind you, but in the Nebraska Cornhuskers, Rockne's Ramblers had a special bugbear. The Huskers had more success against Rockne than any other school, winning three and tying one in eight encounters. Part of the success was simply due to solid football playing; part of it came because of the home field hurdles flung into Notre Dame's path.

A persistent anti-Catholic specter would rear its head when Notre Dame played in Lincoln. Incited by newspaper headlines such as "Horrible Hibernians Invade Today!", students and townsfolk would cluster outside the hotel where the horribles were staying and caterwaul through the night. Banners urging the Cornhuskers to "Beat the Papists" and "Maul the Mackerel-Snappers" saluted the visitors when they walked onto the field.

Invariably, a few of the Nebraska gridders would carry the religious clash into the game. Notre Damers wore medals and scapulars while in uniform, and in the pile-up following a play Husker hands would go for them and try to make the visitors literally choke under pressure. More than one Rambler had his chain yanked noose-tight around his neck. Insults zinged back and forth, escalating into questions of ancestry. And from there into physical rebuttal. After being prodded over the brink, Hunk Anderson growled at one Nebraskan, "I'm not Catholic, but I'm gonna get your Protestant ass anyway!"

The coach scoffed at superstition by wearing a big "13" at practice.

While the ill feelings over religion were an annoying sidelight, they had no real weight in the final score. Nebraska found the key to shackling Notre Dame's speed. That was the difference.

The Cornhusker players fit a general profile: they were tall, strong country boys (as folklore has it, they got their strength by hoisting a newborn calf overhead, and repeating the exercise daily until the animal was a full-grown twelve-hundred pound steer); and most of them were slower than an arthritic mule. On a fast track the Notre Dame backfield could go over, under and around the Nebraska line. No problem. The Huskers called on a little native farming talent, and some good old-fashioned gamesmanship. They doctored their field, slowing down the Irish, giving their big linemen time to lumber in and swat down runners with a calloused paw.

The 1923 game was played on a field of dirt that had been plowed and rolled — but not rolled much. It was unsure footing at best. Every time a Notre Dame back tried to cut upfield his footing gave way like he'd stepped on a pile of marbles. That's the way the gridiron — and the season — crumbled. The Irish suffered their only loss of the year, 14-7.

Two years later, the resourceful Nebraska groundskeeper — presumably an agriculture student who was encouraged to use the field for lab work — let the grass grow to a height of four inches. "Are we going to play football on it, or make it into hay?" asked Rockne. Again the Irish speed was ineffectual. Again the Cornhuskers triumphed, 17-0.

★ ★ ★

How do you get nicknamed "Judge"? If you're Glen "Judge" Carberry you do it by making a fool of yourself in practice.

The Judge.

As a freshman end, Carberry went out for a pass, missed his assignment, and had the quarterback's throw bounce embarrassingly off his noggin. Rockne had been watching. "Carberry!" he barked. "You keep on playing like that and you"ll spend more time on the bench than any judge I know.

The nickname stuck, the absent-minded play did not. "Judge" was a three year letterman at end, and captain of the 1922 squad.

★ ★ ★

In the spring of 1924, May 17 to be exact, the KKK came to town.

The Ku Klux Klan was strong at the time in Indiana; the state's impressionable rural population was easy pickin's for the fear-mongers, the fat-bellied sheriffs and ferret-eyes politicians who realized — much as Hitler did a decade later — that there is strength in paranoia. Throughout the South and Middle West the Klan carried political clout — clout which often dominated local governments and which actually cost Catholic Al Smith the presidential election in 1928.

The students weren't happy about the week-long convention scheduled by the KKK. They didn't see eye-to-hood with the Klan's virulently anti-Catholic ideals, and they did their damndest to subvert the visitors' stay in South Bend.

On the convention's opening day, students dressed as Klansmen stood at highway intersections South of town and shunted incoming KKK traffic onto side roads. Puzzled carloads of Dragons, Kleagles, and assorted half-wits wearing sheets spent the day backtracking through the hamlets of Crumstown, Teegarden and Nappanee.

Other students met arriving Klanners at the train station. When a conventioneer got off the train, a Notre Damer would take him politely by the arm and offer to escort him to his hotel. Down a side street. Into an alley. FOMP! RRRRIP! KOOSH! Waiting allies clobbered the Klanner, defrocked him, and sent him on his way with a swift kick. Production line mugging at its best.

Retaliation came two days later, on Monday, the nineteenth. An anonymous caller tipped off a freshman that a student was getting beaten to death downtown. Word spread across campus like a windswept fire. Soon, despite a directive against such actions from Father Walsh, Notre Dame's president, an angry mob had rallied and headed for town.

The phone call had been a hoax, and the Klan was waiting. South Bend's sheriff, himself a Klansman, had deputized his comrades, now armed with clubs and bottles which they wielded with violent efficiency. The youths from Notre Dame had a bad go of it. Several of them were injured seriously, and were taken to Hullie and Mike's Pool Hall where they rested on the tables, red blood staining the green felt until medical help arrived.

Now the malice was up-front. A riot-sized army of students regrouped back at the campus and marched toward South Bend, bent on croaking the convention, and maybe a few conventioneers in the bargain. They might have done it. More likely, another set of undergraduate heads would have been broken.

Nothing happened.

Father Walsh met the angry young men on the steps of City Hall and spoke the words that dampened their rage: "A single life of a Notre Dame student would be too great a price to pay." Walsh was right and the students knew it. Street-fighting was the Klan's game. The boys fell into neat ranks and trudged back to their dorms.

But Notre Dame administrators remained worried. The KKK would be in town for five more days, and there was no telling what kind of ruckus would hit the wind if some fellow whose hood shrouded a brain with a cantalope's intelligence tried burning a cross at the foot of the Golden Dome. The good Fathers hiked up their cassocks and went into action. Confiscating the hunting guns that many students brought to school, they took them to the fieldhouse, and redistributed them to members of the football and track teams. The athletes were paired into "border patrols." Working in shifts, they comprised a 24-hour guard around the campus perimeter.

Herb Eggert, an engineering student and tackle on the football team, was one of those on patrol. "As I recall, there was a threat to burn down the administration building. That was the main reason we were on those patrols.

"My partner was John Roach — 'Cocky' Roach we called him. We were out real early one morning, just before sunrise, and we hadn't seen anything the least bit mysterious, so we were walking along, making small talk. Then we got out near old Cartier Field. The ticket booths were set out away from the stands in those days. As we passed one of them, we heard a noise inside. Somebody was moving around in there!"

Eggert shakes his head. "Let me tell you, we were scared. We were talking in whispers and waving our guns all over the place, trying to decide what to do. Cocky wanted to riddle the thing with bullets, then look inside. But we decided that I would yank open the door while he kept his gun aimed.

"Both of us," says Eggert, "were certain we'd see a fellow with a sheet and a shotgun."

Roach steadied his gun. Eggert jerked open the door. A crusty old wino, wrapped in newspapers, tumbled out! He had chosen the ticket booth as a secluded spot to sleep off a drunk, and now he awoke to the sight of two gun barrels aimed right between his bloodshot eyes. He must have thought this was a pretty severe penalty for vagrancy.

The week ended without further incident. It's no wonder the footballers had such a good season in 1924. After defensing the Ku Klux Klan, Princeton and Army were cakewalks.

★ ★ ★

The Four Horsemen: Harry Stuhldreher, Don Miller, Jim Crowley and Elmer Layden. A more famous backfield never played the game of football. Together they won twenty-eight games, lost two; in 1924 they set the glorious precedent of rough-riding over everyone to give Notre Dame its first national championship.

Speed, agility, rhythm and deception — these were their weapons.

Especially deception.

Witness how the Horsemen scored their first touchdown.

It was third down and five yards to go for the score. On the sidelines, Knute Rockne was certain it was fourth down. He signalled for a surprising pass.

Quarterback Harry Stuhldreher nodded. Who was he to contradict the great Rockne. Stuhldreher waited until the teams lined up before he remembered Rockne's rule #6 for quarterbacks: "Be boss on offense; you run the team." Rockne or no, Stuhldreher decided to audible a new play, something more appropriate for third down.

As Stuhldreher rattled off the first sequence of numbers, his team shifted. The defense was caught off guard. The right play would bring a score, and Stuhldreher called for that play, barking out the signals for a fullback buck.

This was big news to Elmer Layden, the fullback. Elmer was just catching onto the change in plans when the ball was hiked, banged off his knee, and ricocheted twenty feet into the end zone. George Vergara fell on it for the score.

Maybe the crowd had been chanting, "We Kneed a Touchdown!"

★   ★   ★

Knute Rockne drove a Studebaker. His maid drove a Cadillac. Somewhere, Karl Marx is smiling.

★   ★   ★

A couple of the Rockne kids were snooping around in their father's dresser one morning when little Knute made a pleasant discovery: 500 Notre Dame season football tickets. What a nice gesture it would be, he thought innocently, to give those tickets to his acquaintances at school. So few of them ever got to see Notre Dame play.

Billy and little Knute tucked the tickets away with their lunch and spirited them away to Perley School. At recess the boys stood in the middle of a shrieking flock of children, parceling out the prizes like candy men gone mad. Five here . . . ten there . . . twenty to the girl Billy was sweet on . . . urchins who had come to school with only a sandwich for lunch swaggered home with twenty-five season passes worth five dollars per.

What was the elder Rockne's reaction when he learned that a twenty-five hundred dollar bundle had disappeared, that he'd have to search high and low through the neighborhood to retrieve the tickets?

We will mercifully draw the curtain on that part of the story.

★   ★   ★

One cold and windy South Bend night, miles from Notre Dame, Sleepy Jim Crowley turned a corner and ran smack into the Prefect of Discipline. The priest testily checked his watch. "Crowley," he snapped, "you have three minutes to get back to campus before curfew."

Crowley wetted an index finger and held it aloft. "Don't think I can make it, Father," he deadpanned. "Not against this wind."

★   ★   ★

The only person on the field who noticed the gun was Chuck Collins. As the referee bustled up to spot the ball after a Wisconsin play, the gun, a blank pistol used to signal time, had slipped from his pocket. Collins walked over nonchalantly to where it lay on the turf, picked it up, and tucked it inside his pants.

There are safer activities in this world than playing football with a chunk of metal inside

No, Don Miller's not out of uniform. That's silent movie comedian Snub Pollard with the Three Horsemen.

your pants. Had Collins been hit hard, his anatomy may have carried a permanent engraving of a .22 caliber pistol. But he kept the gun for only a few plays. The Irish got the ball and Jim Crowley soon zipped eighty yards for a touchdown. Collins whipped out the weapon and waltzed over to Doyle Harmon, the Badger captain. "Here Harmon," he chortled, dangling the gun in his opponent's face, "maybe you can stop Crowley with this."

★ ★ ★

It was a beautiful idea. Before the 1924 Army game, star center Adam Walsh pulled the tape off his broken hand. He then bandaged his good hand as though it were the broken one. A wise student of human nature, Adam figured that Army might concentrate on reinjuring the broken hand — anything to knock one of Notre Dame's Seven Mules out of the line-up. Now, with the fractured hand bare and the good hand taped, Army would really be confused.

And they were. The more vicious Cadets left the broken hand alone and stomped and smashed and pounded the bandaged hand until they broke it as well.

Adam played over half the game with two broken hands, snapping every Irish hike with precision and making an important interception in the 13-7 victory.

★ ★ ★

Rip Miller, another of the Seven Mules, enjoyed playing without headgear. Unfortunately, Rip's ears stuck far out from his head, making him look like either Clark Gable or Dumbo in flight, depending upon whose side you were on. To keep from getting his ears torn off during a game, Rip would have to tape them to his head with wide

Comedian Snub Pollard hamming it up for the camera. Adam Walsh finds the football more amusing.

strips of adhesive.

Are you out there, Rip?

Can you hear us?

★ ★ ★

Cocky Roach, true to his name, did not feel appreciated at the University of Wisconsin. After a year of freshman frustration, Cocky pulled his light from under the Badgers' bushel basket and shined it in the direction of Notre Dame. There, his talents were cheered and certain personal quirks, at least tolerated.

Cocky was a better ballplayer than statistics could ever show, since he suffered the misfortune of playing behind the backfield of the Four Horsemen. But you don't need statistics to remember Cocky. There were more than enough memorable incidents in his career, such as the practice in Tucson before the 1925 Rose Bowl. Then Cocky strutted onto the field in a complete cowboy outfit: spurs, chaps, six-shooter, ten-gallon hat, the works. When some coaches asked him to leave, he became indignant. "He almost went for his pistol," remembers a teammate. "And with Cocky, you know it was loaded."

Cocky's best game came against Wisconsin in 1924, when Rockne sent him in to replace Jim Crowley at halfback. On one play, Cocky took the ball on a long streaking run down the sidelines, right past the Wisconsin bench. Still nursing a grudge for his slighted talents, he eyed the captious Wisconsin coaches. He could not hold it in: he thumbed his nose as he ran by. Crossing the goal line, he turned and repeated the gesture for any of the trailing Badger defenders who might have missed it.

Rockne yanked him from the game immediately.

A lot of people mistakenly blamed Jim Crowley for the nose-thumbing. We're happy to set the record straight.

Let's give Cocky credit for something.

★ ★ ★

The 1925 Rose Bowl provided a grand opportunity for the Four Horsemen and Seven Mules, already a smash hit in the East, to strut their stuff out West. They faced Stanford, which boasted a couple of legends itself in Fullback Ernie Nevers and Coach Pop Warner. Nevers was brilliant in the game, running and passing artfully, but his single-handed heroics could not offset the efforts of eleven Notre Damers. The Irish took the game, 27-10.

Notre Dame had never before traveled to the West Coast to play football; Rockne had never seen Stanford play. Yet the team's preparations for the Rose Bowl were so meticulous that they may have had the game in their hip pocket from the opening kick.

Elmer Layden made three interceptions that were crucial to the outcome. Rockne's scouts were responsible. Alumni — most of them former players — had followed Stanford during the year, charting their plays and sending the diagrams to South Bend. The coach ciphered the X's and O's so well tht he anticipated perfectly each time Pop Warner's boys would try a certain sideline pass. He positioned Layden accordingly, and the fullback spent the afternoon plucking footballs away from frustrated receivers. He ran two of the interceptions for TD's of sixty-five and seventy yards.

Rockne was also concerned with getting his squad to Pasadena in peak physical condition. Forewarned by colleagues that a non-stop chug to the coast would weaken the team irreparably, the coach charted a route through New Orleans, Houston, El Paso, and Tucson. Theoretically, this would ease the strain on the players and allow them to get acclimated to warm weather. Practically, the roundabout route meant that practices could be conducted away from prying eyes; and the shifting scenery kept the team from jading during the layoff from competition.

There was also a problem with water. The water in towns along the way surely contained rebellious bacteria. Rockne wanted his backfield doing the Notre Dame shift, not the Green Apple Two-Step. So he packed a baggage car on the train with good ol' Notre Dame water. Whether it was touring the French Quarter or practicing on a high school field in Houston, the Notre Dame entourage was shadowed dutifully by a student manager in a taxicab jammed full of water jugs.

The Rose Bowl was a successful foray for the Irish on more accounts than the final score. The Horsemen, the Mules, and the ever-charming Rockne won legions of new followers in a growing region of the country. And of course the Holy Cross Fathers banked a big green jackpot.

A couple of interesting postscripts:

Two days after the game, Jim Crowley nearly died. The team train was bound for San Francisco for a few days of sightseeing when Crowley suddenly turned deathly white, collapsed, and stopped breathing. Father O'Hara, the team chaplain, performed mouth-to-mouth resuscitation and also administered last rites of the Catholic Church. Momentarily, the halfback was breathing again, and after one day in a hospital he was fit to rejoin the team. His illness was officially termed "acute indigestion." Suspicions linger that he was actually smitten by a bug known as the Revenge of the Bootlegger.

And the saga of the Rose Bowl would not be complete without mention of Leo Sutliffe. Leo was Notre Dame's student manager, and as such he was responsible for the team's expenses during the trip. When he returned to campus in January he submitted his expense sheet to the university bookkeeper. It read:

Money received: $15,000
Money spent: 14,985
Money returned: 15

This, of course, was an accountant's nightmare. The bookkeeper was outraged. "No good! No good!" he sputtered. You've got to have everything itemized. I need to see receipts. Now get out of here, and don't come back until you can account for every penny!"

Leo tramped out. He hadn't fussed with receipts, and to recollect every expenditure during the three-week trip was an impossibility. He was in a bind. Then he snapped his fingers — the solution was obvious.

Twenty minutes later he walked into the bookkeeper's cubbyhole and slapped down the same expense sheet. The clerk nearly bit through his fountain pen. He'd never met such impudence from a student! He picked up the sheet, fully intending to stick it in an orifice of Sutliffe's body, then looked at it closely, swallowed hard, and slumped back in his chair. "I guess this'll be allright," he murmured.

What the bookkeeper had seen were the initials "KKR" scrawled across the paper. Leo had gone to Rockne and had him okay the accounting. Checkmate.

Leo Sutliffe, where are you today? The Teamster's Pension Fund is looking for a few good men.

★ ★ ★

The Rose Bowl itself was one of those odd contests in which the offensive leader winds up on the wrong end of the final score. Stanford beat Notre Dame in first downs, seventeen to seven, and in yards gained, 298 to 179. Only in points did the Irish come out on top. The lopsided stats made Stanford the game's real victor, someone suggested.

"Sure," answered Sleepy Jim Crowley, "and next year the major leagues will start awarding baseball games to the team with the most men left on base."

★ ★ ★

The Irishmen got a big break when Stanford's Bill Solomon fumbled a punt that Notre Dame's Ed Hunsinger alertly fielded and ran in for a touchdown.

"What a jerk I am," moaned the anguished Solomon, beating his fists into the ground. "What an idiot! I have got to be the worst . . ."

"Solomon," said Crowley, "you can shut up. Nobody's arguing with you."

★ ★ ★

Stanford adherents still claim that the turning point of the game came when Cardinal Fullback Ernie Nevers was stopped short of the goal line after a desperate fourth down plunge. According to this tired alibi, Never undoubtedly scored the touchdown, but the @#★*† referee incorrectly spotted the ball eight inches away from paydirt.

"I had great seats," a man in a bar fumed some years later. "I seen the whole thing. We got cheated. Nevers was in the end zone."

"He was not," came a voice from the other end of the bar.

"Oh yeah? Where were you sitting?"

"I'm Harry Stuhldreher," said the voice. "I was sitting on Nevers' head."

★ ★ ★

After the success of the 1924 season, the Four Horsemen, including Elmer Layden, were invited to audition for the Balabon and Katz theater chain in Chicago. The boys arrived in the Windy City one day in Holy Week and limped through a few hours of uninspiring rehearsals. The famous four were about as underwhelming as a backfield of Al Jolsen, Eddy Cantor, Georgie Jessel and Sophie Tucker would have been on the gridiron. Before they left, the Horsemen were herded into a photographer's studio to pose with chorus girls for some publicity stills.

Elmer Layden was worried all the way back to school. It was bad enough to look ridiculous on stage. Now there were these publicity pictures to deal with. The girls in them were dressed as all chorus girls dress: the minute you saw them, you had one thing on your mind. Elmer remembered that it was Holy Week. If the priests at Notre Dame ever see those pictures, he thought, they'll toss us out of school. As soon as he got back to South Bend, Elmer phoned the theater people and told them to forget it.

So much for Elmer Layden's vaudeville career.

A few years later, Elmer was called to Hollywood to act in a movie, *The Spirit of Notre Dame,* an Irish setter if ever there was one. Elmer never quite got over it. He played himself in the picture, but got paid as an extra. For the rest of his life he had people phoning him in the wee hours of the morning, waking him up and bubbling, "Guess who I just saw on the late show?!" After the first fifty or so, these calls are not nearly as exciting as they sound.

So much for Elmer Layden's movie career.

That's showbiz. Elmer Layden egg.

★ ★ ★

The Four Horsemen: Layden, Crowley, Miller, Stuhldreher. Elmer's the only one that didn't get a leather jacket.

During the first half of the 1926 Minnesota game, Joe Boland was trying to block a punt when his leg was broken by his own teammate. Fred Collins suffered a multiple jaw fracture on the next play, and the two left the field in the same ambulance.

★ ★ ★

If you had to pick someone from your high school class who was going to spend his college years worrying about choreography, who would it be? Probably that skinny kid with the spectacles who sat by the window, huh? Or the vice-president of the drama club, you know, the guy who couldn't grow hair on his legs. Anybody but the fellows in the letter sweaters, right?

Wrong. At least as far as Rockne was concerned. Rock demanded of his players, especially of his backs, the grace and agility of professional dancers. The Monogram Absurdities, an annual stage farce of singing and dancing student-athletes, was many times the excuse Rockne used to put his charges under the tutelage of a dance instructor. While the players learned a few steps for the stage, they absorbed a smoothness of motion that might later prove invaluable on the field.

Prevailing pigskin philosophy insists that the only real winners are those boring machines that stick to plodding fundamentals. Rockne would have cringed. In his day, a football coach courted public opinion, not flouted it. Always the showman, he choreographed plays that befuddled opponents as well as suited the fans' tastes for flashy football. He paced his attack like a Broadway show. The mainspring of his offense, the backfield shift, was nothing less than a graceful, rhythmic football dance.

Rockne's detractors always note that he didn't invent the shift. It's like saying J. D. Rockefeller didn't invent the oil business. After a few years of experimentation, Rockne retooled the primitive shift he had inherited from Jesse Harper into the most baffling and powerful offense ever seen.

Now, technical descriptions of football are, on par, about as interesting as *Your Toaster and How it Works*. The Notre Dame shift, however, bears explanation.

The backs lined up in straight T-formation behind a balanced line and shifted left or right to the count of three, usually regrouping in the shape of a box. At the quarterback's signal, the backs counted: "one" — took a step; "two" — jumped into position; "three" — sprang forward at the hike.

The rhythm of the shift was swift, hypnotic, precise; the backs' movements perfectly synchronized. All four shifted with identical actions, all moving as one man. There was never any clue as to who was going to get the ball and where he was going to run. More than discombobulating a defense, the shift worked because Rockne's backs went barreling into the line with a bundle of momentum built up from all that swirling around.

Notre Dame's opponents, many of them helpless before the swift and rhythmic Rockne offense, and not blessed with the talent to shift to the shift themselves, decided to switch battlegrounds. The idea seemed to be, if you can't beat them on the field, legislate them off it. The rules that govern backfield-in-motion today are direct descendants of those stopgap measures instituted to slow down Notre Dame.

The shift was so fast that a back never seemed to stand still. So, in 1920, the rulesmakers decreed that backs had to have both feet stationary before the snap of the ball. This had all the effect of pouring high octane on a bonfire.

Some officials believed that Rockne's offense

The Babe outfitting a friend.

worked within the rules; just as many did not. And almost every opposing coach claimed foul whenever the Irish backs shifted into high gear. It was the popular thing to do.

Referees at the 1921 Nebraska game just stopped trying to figure out what was going on in the Notre Dame backfield, and penalized the Irish over two-hundred yards in a weary effort to get the game back to normal. Two games later, Army Mentor Charley Daly complained so bitterly against the shift that Rockne handicapped himself, ordering his quarterback to call every play in the second half from short punt formation. Army didn't stop grousing until they unleashed their own version of the shift against Navy and bested the Middies 7 to zip.

In 1922, Notre Dame's opponents pushed through a rule demanding a full stop in the backfield so that all momentum was lost. A "sufficient pause" was supposed to mark this full stop. What was

sufficient? Rockne squawked that, for his opponents, it was just long enough for a defensive adjustment.

But as for stopping momentum, the Irish coach got around that easily enough. His backs leaped into position on "two" and swung their bodies to the side, then forward at the snap, like four strong saplings, bent back and suddenly let loose.

This ended in 1926. An absolute stop was decreed. Swinging and swaying specifically outlawed. Not enough. In 1927, the legislators demanded that (except for a man in motion parallel to the line) backs remain stationary for one second. In case of doubt, officials were instructed to call the penalty. And a shifting team forfeited fifteen yards for illegal motion; a non-shifting team only five.

How it all irritated Rockne! "Football wasn't made for any defensive team," he howled. "But if they keep changing the rules, I'll change too. From the cut of speedy, intelligent, capable players I now

coach to the ones with bovine expressions and ox-knuckle ankles, the hippopotamus-catching players that so many schools use today."

By the way, to help gauge the elapsed second between shift and snap, the rulesmakers advised the referees to count quickly: "One-two-three-four."

"That's dandy," said Rockne. "But what if the referee stutters?"

★　★　★

Halftime of the 1927 Minnesota game.

Golden Gopher Coach Doc Spears had assembled his team for a pep talk when through the walls came the blaring staccato of Knute Rockne's voice. What mesmerizing oratory! A wall away, Rock blasted and fired his players; the Minnesota squad sat at hushed attention. When the long harrangue ended, Doc Spears stared hard at his team and shouted: "You heard what he said. Now go out and do that to Notre Dame!"

Final score, fittingly enough, a 7-7 tie.

★　★　★

That was the year the Irish saw red against Army. Specifically, the red was in the face of Light Horse Harry Wilson, the Army halfback who blushed quite visibly every time he knew he would be carrying the ball. The Notre Dame defense operated on the simple principle of smothering the man with the stoplight face. When Wilson took his stance under normal coloring, the Notre Damers ignored him and concentrated on tackling his companions. The Irish should have known better than to judge a man by the color of his skin. Army whitewashed them, 18-0.

★　★　★

The most famous athlete ever to wear a Notre Dame football uniform never played football for Notre Dame. He was Babe Ruth, shown here chucking a southpaw spiral as the boys look on.

The persuasiveness of Rockne's oratory is probably best illustrated by the case of John Dugan. It really was a case, a legal one.

Despite the fact that the United States was locked in the dry grip of Prohibition, Dugan managed to celebrate one Irish victory in style. After slipping into a South Bend speakeasy, he drank more than enough bathtub gin to gum up his own plumbing and, with curfew approaching, decided to take a streetcar back to campus.

Dugan took that streetcar. Well, actually, he stole one that had been parked for the night. At least that was the way the arresting officers saw it. *Somebody* had to drive," explained our hero.

Sobered up and hauled before the court, Dugan could offer no defense. It was a clear case of Halloweening out of season; he could only argue for mercy. Better yet, why not have Rockne argue for mercy? Dugan began speaking to the judge with the mannerisms and in the voice of Rockne, an imitation he had been perfecting for months. Impressed or amused, the judge dropped all charges.

It's an old saying, but it probably fits no one better than John Dugan: when he imitates a bird, you don't dare look up.

★ ★ ★

The team's almost purely Protestant schedules were no accident. Rockne was well aware of Notre Dame's lofty standing with American Catholics and of the school's commensurate financial gains. Except for occasional "share the wealth" games against Marquette, St. Louis, or Loyola, Rockne was not about to divide anyone's loyalties.

Which reminds us of a story, as the day's vaudevillians used to say. A Catholic school is playing a Protestant one. After a couple of scrimmages the Protestant captain protests that the Catholics are biting in the pile-ups.

"It's not easy to detect an occasional nip in such circumstances," says the ref, "but I'll try."

A few more minutes of action, and the Protestant captain reports: "I have teeth marks all over me! Those Catholics won't stop biting us!"

"Son," says the referee, "you should have scheduled them for a Friday."

★ ★ ★

Chuck Collins played left end with only three fingers on one hand.

His brother Fred played fullback with only one lung.

★ ★ ★

George Vlk, an end on the 1928-1930 teams, was hit so hard during one scrimmage he had all the vowels knocked out of his last name.

★ ★ ★

Spearheaded by a group of Eastern universities who were fading from gridiron prominence, there was a late-twenties drive to de-emphasize college football. Scuttle scholarships! Wreck recruiting! Trim travel! Phase football back to the clubby status it held at the turn of the century — when the East dominated the game, naturally.

The National Football Rules Committee (forerunner to the NCAA), a puppet of Eastern athletic directors, had raised Rockne's hackles several times by tampering with the shift. Then there were other developments that he saw as boding ill for football: Yale signed agreements with its opponents for the 1927 season to ban all forms of scouting; a Dartmouth committee proposed that coaches be banned from the sidelines and exiled to a seat in the stands; and a Carnegie Commission study in 1929 cited high injury rates and creeping professionalism, and suggested that the college game be abolished completely.

The Notre Dame coach knew there were problems, especially with illicit recruiting, but he considered them curable growing pains of a great sport. At a 1927 banquet in Dallas he busted out with the opening statement in what would become a personal crusade to preserve the game. Decrying the "effete easterners," he charged that ". . . they are trying to change the game from a he-man's sport into a silk stocking contest . . . . It is too rough for them . . . . They are hoping to regain their superiority, which they held for a long period when the game was in its infancy."

Verbal jousting between the Irish coach and members of the Eastern press — who ran headlines such as "Rockne's Farcial Charges" — continued until his death in 1931. At every opportunity Rockne took a soapbox to lambast the Rules Committee or the Carnegie Commission's proposals.

In 1927, at halftime of the Southern Cal game in Soldier Field, he helped stage a burlesque football game to show fans just where the sport was heading. Billed as a "football contest of the future," the event bordered on the bizarre.

Two teams, the "Rough-necks" and the "Tiller Boys," took the field clad in assorted ballet tutus, lace gowns and frilly petticoats, and pranced into formation. (The participants were men.) The ball was hiked and the carrier walted on his tip-toes until he was tagged by an opposing player.

Play continued in this dainty fashion until the ref tinkled a bell — tea time! Tables and chairs were hustled onto the grid. The teams sat down together to exchange crumpets and social amenities.

There were 120,000 people in the stands. Maybe ten of them caught the satire.

Dick Halpin, class of 1927, who assisted Rockne in organizing the show: "I waved the boys off after a couple of minutes. Oh, golly, we were making fools of ourselves! I was on the sideline going, 'C'mon, get off, get off!' None of the fans knew what was going on. Boy," smiled Halpin, still sheepish at the memory after fifty years, "it sure didn't have the effect Rock had planned."

A favorite Rockne speech described his prospective report of the 1935 Northwestern-Notre Dame game. It may have been extravagant exaggeration, but the target was squarely between the cross hairs:

"Receiving at fullback for Northwestern," he said the report would read, "was M. Bickerdash Pix III of the famous North Shore family. The entire Northwestern team was gaily clad in purple-mauvette tunics, and about the waist was a white girdle with a Louis XIV buckle.

"Kicking off for Notre Dame was T. Fitzpatrick Murphy, who is better known to his cronies as Two Lump becuase he always asks for two lumps of sugar in his orange pekoe. The Notre Dame team also presented a striking appearance with their green shirtwaists and their headgear resembling a woodsman's toque. Giving a very neat appearance without being at all gaudy was the fact that their hip pads were trimmed with georgette. Hanging from their necks were pendants, lavalliere type, on which were engraved the motto of the University: *Fight fairly but furiously.*

And so it would go, with a fifteen-minute description of the game. Finally, he would have M. Bickerdash Pix III break loose down the field, with only "Two Lump" between him and the goal.

"But did Two Lump become panicky and give up?" Rockne would ask. "Not old Two Lump. With a *savoire faire* for which he was justly famous, he cupped his hand and he called in a loud voice that could be heard all over the amphitheater:

'I say, Bickerdash, old thing, there's a terrible run in your stocking,'

"Imagine the intense embarrassment and mortification of poor old Bickerdash. What could he do to hide his discomfiture but drop the ball and sneak away to the clubhouse, and the game was saved."

Ah, if only the coach could have stayed around to see modern-day All-Americans George Goeddeke and Ross Browner. Goeddeke was 6'3", 230 lbs.; Browner was 6'4", 250. Both sported an earring on occasion.

What would Rock have said?

One look, and he would probably have asked them to, uh, please pass the tea.

★ ★ ★

"We must guard against those who would turn football into a game for sissies."
— **K. K. Rockne**

Somedays, your best should be better.

"Hoffman!" bellowed Knute Rockne. Nordy Hoffman, who had seen precious little playing time, grabbed his helmet. He flew to the side of his coach.

"Get in there and block that kick," ordered the Rock.

"Yes sir." Nordy rushed into the game and took his place against the opponent's punting formation. The ball was snapped. Two lines crunched together. Nordy Hoffman banged, squeezed, and broke free. He thrust his hands up the instant the ball flew off the punter's foot. There was a loud swat, a numbing fire in Hoffman's fingers. The kick was blocked! Notre Dame recovered.

Justifiably proud, Nordy hitched up his trousers and prepared to dig in for more action. Suddenly, he felt a teammate's tap on the shoulder. "I'm in for you," he was told.

Dejected, confused, Nordy jogged back to the sidelines. "Now," said Rock, "if you learn to block offensively, I'll play you all the time."

★ ★ ★

One big lineman won a place on the team though he had never before played football. He started out as a student manager, assigned to retrieve the heavy iron ball of the shot-put for the hulking musclemen at track practice. "I got tired of carrying it back," remembers the lineman. "So I started to roll it. Then I just started throwing it back. And when I was tossing it over the shot-putters heads, well, the coaches figured they had to get me into uniform for *some* sport. And that sport was football."

Why not track?

"Throwing an iron ball isn't half as much fun as throwing a quarterback."

★ ★ ★

There are always those who manage to lean defiantly against the winds of change. Take Jack Cannon. Jack was the last man at Notre Dame to play football without headgear. Bareheaded, he manned a left guard position for the 1929 team. Cannon was good, too. In fact, he was an All-American.

Though he sometimes had trouble remembering what day it was.

★ ★ ★

In sharp contrast to today's coaches, Knute Rockne tried to dissuade his charges from playing pro ball. If they wanted a career in football, Rockne steered them toward coaching. He did a pretty good job of it. Eighty-nine of his players followed his advice and example.

One of them, Harry Mehre, was thrilled to sign a rare lifetime contract to coach the Universiy of Mississippi. In spite of the contract's terms, Mehre was eventually fired.

How could that happen, he was asked.

"Simple," replied Mehre. "They just declared me legally dead."

★ ★ ★

"Horse" Mehre — reports of his death were premature.

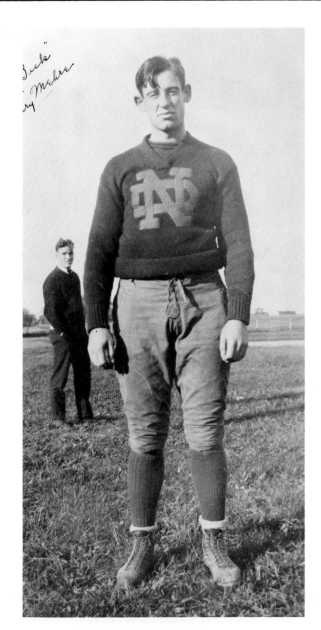

Law of Sing-Sing.

John Law, captain of the 1929 National Champions, was another Domer who became a coach. Maybe it was his name, more likely it was his background — Law was hired for the head job at Sing-Sing Prison. Consider the traditional coaching headaches he avoided:

Every policeman in the country recruited for him.

He never lost anyone because of grades.

Training was simple; the only bars were in the windows.

The alumni never came back to haunt him on weekends.

He got to play all his games at home.

★ ★ ★

Years after Clipper Smith retired from coaching, he was asked if he missed the game.

"I did at first," he admitted. "But there's something I'll never miss. You can't imagine what it's like having to sit there and watch an eighteen-year-old kid run onto the field with your paycheck fluttering between his fingers."

★ ★ ★

Rockne's most successful pupil, Frank Leahy, was often accused of driving hurt and exhausted players. But Leahy never asked anything he did not expect of himself.

In the 1929 Army game, Leahy dislocated his right elbow, and wore a cast for the next three weeks. When the plaster came off, the doctors told the scrappy tackle to forget about football for the year. Instead, Leahy promptly forgot what the doctors told him, and reported to Rockne.

"Frank, how's that elbow?" The coach was concerned.

"Wonderful, Rock. I'll be able to play this week."

"That's not what the doctors say. Let's see you flex it."

Leahy could feel his right elbow throb at the mere mention of being moved. So he flung out his left arm: twirled it, flexed it, moved it up and down like a contortionist.

If Rockne knew that Leahy was using his good arm, he never let on. "You know, Frank," he shook his head, "those doctors keep telling me I'm washed up too. We'll show them."

Leahy started in the next game, playing with an elbow that could not push open a swinging door.

★ ★ ★

The next year, Leahy reinjured a bad knee playing tiddlywinks on a kitchen floor.

★ ★ ★

When the 1929 Ramblers arrived to play Indiana University, they were held up at the gate.

"Can't get in without a pass," said a student manager, officiously blocking the doorway.

"But we're Notre Dame!" blurted Rockne.

"I ain't supposed to let anybody in. That's orders."

"Boys," Rockne shouted to his team. "this is going to be easier than we thought. They aren't expecting us."

★ ★ ★

"I tell you, Knute Rockne's name will live when the following generation can't tell you whether Nicolas Murray Butler was an educator or a politician."

— Will Rogers, 1930.

Well, next generation, who was Nicholas Murray Butler?

★   ★   ★

Moon Mullins, on playing for Rockne: "You'd practice 'till your fingernails sweat."

★   ★   ★

Maybe the most enduring image of Knute Rockne is that of the master psychologist. His rallying cry for the 1928 Army game, "Win one for The Gipper," needs no ballyhooing here. Other halftime talks, not so well documented and perhaps apocryphal, are almost as famous. "Let's go girls," was the complete text of one. "Fighting Irish? Bah!" was another. The coach waxed more expansive at the midpoint of the 1925 Northwestern game: "You can tell your grandchildren you had the honor of playing on the first team to quit at Notre Dame." So saying, Rock abandoned his players for a seat in the stands. But he was back on the sidelines by the fourth quarter to see Notre Dame nail down the 13-10 victory.

The impression then is of Rockne, the locker room psychologist. But that is unfair. This was a man who could tailor any ego to fit his team, could turn any emotional situation to his benefit. His last game went far beyond the bounds of stirring pep talks. It was psychological warfare from start to finish.

★

By December there were no words left for the 1930 USC Trojans. "The Wonder Boys" they were called, the best the West had ever seen. They did, indeed, seem unstoppable, blowing top-rate opponents off the field by incredibly lopsided scores: 32-0, 52-0, 74-0. What would it be against Notre Dame?

Rockne's Ramblers were figured to be overrated. The defending national champs and winners of eighteen in a row were visibly weary. Two tough, tight games against Army and Northwestern had wasted the team to its breaking point. And with Savoldi and Mullins out of the line-up, there was no fullback in sight to plug that gaping hole in the Irish backfield.

Why bother with alibis? Every sportswriter in the country agreed that USC could not be beaten, whomever the opponent. Rockne himself as much as admitted impending disaster. "We're not giving up the ship," he sighed a week before the game. "but we're prepared to man the lifeboats."

The Notre Dame Special chugged out of Chicago's LaSalle Street Station on 9:30 of a Tuesay evening, November 30. In his private compartment Rockne sat, stuck his chin in his hand, stared out the black window, and plotted. Within the next few days, he would orchestrate the emotions of thousands of people, and spring an unprecedented hoax on the entire nation.

★

The con job started as soon as the Ramblers arrived in Tucson for Wednesday and Thursday workouts, standard procedure for a Notre Dame team traveling to the coast. Rockne's first problem was to find a fullback. Advice was plentiful: every newspaper in America had already announced that Dan Hanley was the only logical choice. Rockne, however, decided to gamble, and stuck third-string halfback Bucky O'Connor into the starting fullback spot. The difficult assignments and precise rhythms of Rockne's ever-shifting backfield made this sort of reassignment impossible, which is probably why the coach decided to keep it a secret.

Very quietly, Rockne had Hanley and O'Connor switch jerseys. The whole team was in on the gag when O'Connor impersonated Hanley at Wednesday's practice. Play after play, the transplanted halfback plowed unimpressively into the middle of the line, never once flashing his brilliant outside speed. Los Angeles sportswriters yawned and wired back reports that Rockne's backfield was indeed in trouble. Like Will Rogers, and much to Rockne's delight, Southern Cal knew only what they read in the newspapers. Two years earlier the West Coast scribes had described Notre Dame's Tucson practices in such detail that Rock blamed them for his team's 27-14 defeat. Now the writers were on his side, if unwittingly.

Bill Henry of the *Los Angeles Times* actually interviewed Hanley (nee O'Connor) after the Wednesday scrimmage. O'Connor obligingly answered every question without stirring the slightest suspicion. Rockne, it seems, had coached him on Hanley's background the night before.

When the reporters demanded a prediction, Rock was uncharacteristically glum. He expected to lose by two touchdowns. But the familiar grin had to be bursting behind the coach's unhappy mask. The switch had gone off without a hitch.

★

"Men will work twice as hard under the stress of emotion as they would otherwise," Rockne had once written. Now he proceeded to prove it.

Nordy Hoffman, Marty Brill, and Tom Conley decided to dress early for Thursday morning's practice. The Arizona fieldhouse was open, but the door to the dressing room was jammed shut.

"Must be locked," Hoffman told his teammates.

"Let's wait outside." The three bounced cheerfully down a dark hallway to a door opening onto a bright, sunny field. Purple mountains loomed in the distance, an intoxicating view. This seemed the ideal place to wait for the locker room to open.

Other players arrived, joining the men on the meadow. No sense bothering with the dressing room; the place was sure to be locked, what with fellows lounging about in street clothes, taking in the sights.

Most of the squad was working on a little applied geometry — "how far away do you suppose those mountains are?" — when Rockne suddenly appeared five minutes before the scheduled start of practice. "What's the idea?" The coach had never looked angrier. "Not a one of you dressed and on the field!"

"The door's locked," someone volunteered.

"That door is not locked," Rockne seethed.

A few players rushed inside. "It's open," came the cry, followed by a stampede for the lockers. No one can strip, slip into pads, tape up, lace up, pull on a uniform, and be ready for football inside of five minutes. It is doubly impossible when surrounded by a bundle of beefy ballplayers attempting the very same thing. But the entire Notre Dame team did it that day, scrambling to the field as if the dressing room had been on fire.

Embarrassed, the Irish hustled through the motions. Rockne was not buying. He sourly called the team together and announced his resignation. "Forget it," he thundered. "I'm out here against doctor's orders, risking my life with this phlebitis, and you numbskulls can't even get to practice on time. It's obvious you don't care about a thing. You don't care about yourselves or your team. So forget it. I'm taking the next train back to Chicago. Coach yourselves. Or get somebody else to do it. I'm a sick man, and I've had it."

Rockne, as it turns out, was almost surely responsible for the locked dressing room; but his players would not realize that until weeks later. Now they simply believed they were being abandoned.

The coach turned to leave. Someone blurted. "Give us another chance, Rock." Everyone chimed in: "Another chance!" One player loudly insisted that Rock had to be present when the team "beat hell out of Southern Cal."

At first, like the locker room door, Rockne could not be moved. Then he seemed to sway a bit. The pleading continued and finally the coach held up his hand.

"One last chance," he said. "Maybe. I'll be back here at one o'clock to quiz you on your assignments. I won't be associated with anyone who doesn't know exactly what he has to do when the ball is snapped."

With that Parthian shot, he disappeared.

A leisurely lunch did not ensue. Each player was expected to know every defensive set, every offensive play his team could use. The mountains seemed too far away and unimportant now. Everyone was cramming.

Rockne arrived promptly after lunch and quizzed everyone orally: "You, think fast, what would you do in this situation? Why? Take the man on your right, what will he be doing and how can you compensate?"

The questions reeled on. Two hours later, the coach seemed satisfied. Everyone had passed. There would be no more talk of returning to Chicago.

★

Practice ended that afternoon when Line Coach Hunk Anderson read aloud a wire service news story about Tom Lieb, another Notre Dame assistant who had recently moved to California. Popular, much-admired, Lieb was every player's friend; thus did the story shock so deeply. Lieb had predicted the winner of Saturday's game: Southern Cal, hands down.

Lieb (at Rockne's secret behest) argued that Notre Dame was fat, injured, slow, worn down and totally incapable of handling the Trojans for an instant. The team listened to Hunk's recitation — duly punctuated with vivid obscenities — and felt betrayed. The betrayal triggered anger. Now the Irish knew they had to win.

★

The team that steamed out of Tucson on Friday morning was riding high. Rockne's threatened walk-out — put on or not — had touched a nerve. The O'Connor-Hanley exchange was so bizarre it jangled the team's guts like a ticking time bomb. Lieb's prediction was a shot of adrenalin. Rockne had switched on his team's emotions like an electric current.

Notre Dame arrived in Los Angeles to the sound of sirens. A police escort met the Ramblers at Union Station and led team buses up Sixth Street to the Ambassador Hotel. Rockne seemed unusually unnerved by a small crowd of well-wishers and reporters waiting in the lobby. "No one speaks," he warned his players, and shunted them upstairs to their rooms.

He did not leave them locked up for long. Several secret meetings were called throughout the day. Players were pulled out of their rooms and sent to the coach to learn of yet another new play, or a suddenly discovered chink in the USC armor. So much fresh material was presented that the players barely had time to worry about their old assignments, which was precisely Rockne's idea.

★

The improbable drama climaxed that evening at a giant USC pep rally where Rockne graciously agreed to address the Trojans. His message was simple: We know how good you are. Don't beat us too badly, and we'll try to give you a better game next year.

"It will be no disgrace to lose to a team with such spirit," announced the coach. "I have warned my boys against over-ambition. We are not over-ambitious in the game. There is room at the top for only one great team."

The Trojans listened intently and liked what they heard. After the rally, they floated away convinced of their greatness, assured of victory. Not a one of them noticed the trap, the Trojan horse of complacency that Rockne had wheeled into their collective subsconscious.

★

Nearly 100,000 people squeezed into the Los Angeles Coliseum that Saturday to see Notre Dame's shame. Back in the locker room, the kick-off fast approaching, Rockne chalked still another new play on the board, a deceptive pass he insisted would go for a touchdown. Then he played his last psychological card.

"You all know that Moon here is from Alhambra, just a few miles away." Rock touched the shoulder of the likable fullback whose bandaged knee had sentenced him to the bench. "Moon's friends and family are here, sitting in the stands. They want Moon in the line-up and so do I. Now, if you players can get us a fourteen point lead by halftime, Moon goes in."

The locker room erupted. There was no more popular man on the squad than Moon.

"Just get those fourteen points," cried Rockne, and his team burst onto the field determined to play their popular friend into action. A quick pass, the one that Rockne had just outlined, made it 7-0. The "66-2 reverse" to O'Connor, whom almost everyone still thought was Hanley, resulted in an eighty-yard streaking touchdown. The dizzy USC players looked like small boys who had just smoked their first cigars.

The prescribed 14-0 halftime score allowed Rockne to start the third quarter by sending Moon Mullins limping in for one play as the crowd roared. The rest of the day was Notre Dame's; final score, 27-0. The "Wonder Team" had all Winter to wonder what went wrong.

★

Everyone was stung by this one. The sportswriters who looked silly for trumpeting USC's invincibility lost all semblance of credibility when it was learned that Rockne had pulled the O'Connor-Hanley switch right before their unseeing eyes. The USC players had been floating on a sea of praise all season; Rockne tipped them over and watched them sink. The Notre Dame team was shamed, angered, pumped up into giving an unbeatable performance. Looking back, it is obvious that Rockne expected to win all the time.

It was the master psychologist's last national championship.

His last game.

His finest.

★ ★ ★

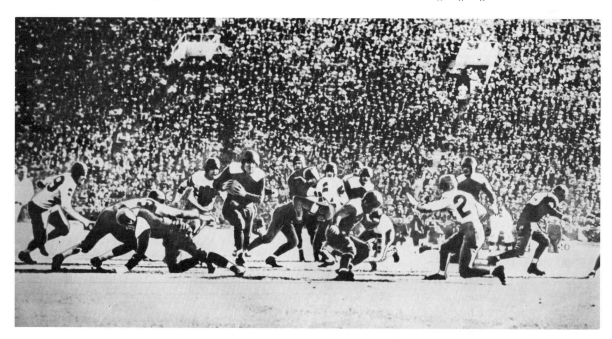

The beginning of Bucky's 80-yard burst.

The complete football player must be able to take punishment as well as dish it out. Here Rockne demonstrates for Coach 'Pop' Warner.

The master conducts a summer coaching clinic.

The six-cylinder *Rockne* rolled out of Studebaker's South Bend plant soon after the coach's death. Rockne's widow, Bonnie, is inspecting the engine.

IV.

Some Gems From the Rock

and

A Peek in the Coach's Briefcase

Rockne had a notable flair for epigrams. Herewith a few Gems from the Rock:

One loss is good for the soul. Too many losses are not good for the coach.

Egotism is the anesthetic that deadens the pain of stupidity.

(On the best way to stop a charging lineman) Give him a scrapbook.

(On the sport of hockey at Notre Dame) It doesn't seem like a good idea to me, putting clubs into the hands of so many Irishmen.

Humility is the lesson every athlete must learn in secret commune with his soul — or he gets it in big sour doses on the field as thousands roar.

You can't be a football player and a lover too.

Never ridicule a beginner — you can kill talent before it blossoms.

The result of any vote on a football team will always be seven to four.

Freshmen get nothing but abuse at Notre Dame — but plenty of that.

The qualifications for a lineman are to be big and dumb. The qualifications for a backfield man are just to be dumb.

Outside the Church, the best thing we've got is good, clean football.

(On cocktails) Drink the first, sip the second, skip the third.

The one thing no one can ever take away from you is your integrity.

The secret of winning football is this: Work more as a team, less as individuals. It play not my eleven best, but my best eleven.

One oration a season is quite enough for any football squad. If a coach talks too much, his words lose weight.

The toughest poison a coach has to face in football is overconfidence.

I can tell you something twelve times. After that, you're on your own.

When in doubt, punt.

Even on the road, his mind was on the field.

He exchanged plays and ideas with hundreds of coaches.

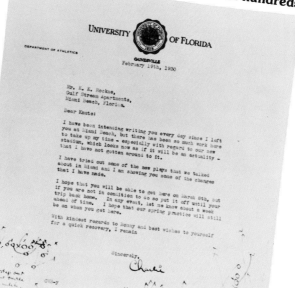

Graphic advice for his players.

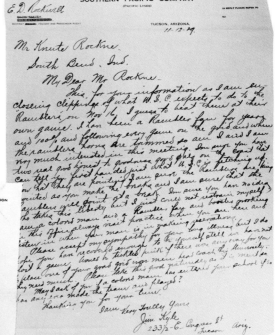

Fan letters.

Fan letters.

A PEEK IN THE COACH'S BRIEFCASE

Most of the coach's personal effects were burned after Mrs. Rockne's death — an effort by his daughter to keep some corner of privacy in the life of this extremely public man.

But a leather satchel packed with Rockne's papers escaped the flames. Gathering dust and mildew, it had sat in a garage in Southern Michigan, unnoticed for years. During 1977, we were given access to the briefcase, we sorted through it, and here is some of what we found:

Notes on psychology; new plays.

UNIVERSITY OF NOTRE DAME
ATHLETIC ASSOCIATION
NOTRE DAME, INDIANA

KNUTE K. ROCKNE
DIRECTOR OF ATHLETICS

Nervous player — Too High Strung — Keep him out of game until second quarter or tell him Wednesday he is not going to play, so he won't worry.

Phlegmatic type — Tell him just before important game that students think he is yellow.

Some hints in values for Offensive Quarter Back

V A L U E

Line Plunge (2 yds. - 3 out of 4.
            (no gain - 1 out of 4.

Slant (3 yds. - 3 out of 4.
      (no gain - 1 out of 4.

Flank Play (4 yds. - 2 out of 4.
           (no gain - 1 out of 4.
           (Lose 2 yds. - 1 out of 4.

Forward Pass -
Long (Complete 4 out of 8.
     (Incomplete 2 out of 8.
     (Intercepted 2 out of 8.

Short (Complete 6 out of 8.
      (Incomplete 1 out of 8.
      (Intercepted 1 out of 8.

Punt → Should average 40 yds

USE ALPHA CEMENT
ALPHA PORTLAND CEMENT
ALPHA PORTLAND CEMENT

Schedule 1930
Indiana   Notre Dame
Navy   Notre Dame Oct 11
Drake   Notre Dame Nov 15
S Cal   Notre Dame Oct 4
So Cal   Los Angeles Dec 5
Pitt at   Pitt Oct 25
N W at   Evanston Nov 22
Army at   N.Y. City Nov 29
Penn   at Philadelphia Nov 8
1931
Pitt   at Notre Dame Oct 24
Penn   at Notre Dame Nov 7
N W   at Notre Dame
S Cal   at Notre Dame Nov 21
Army   at N Y City Nov 28
               at Baltimore Oct 10

Snapshots from a day on the links — rare relaxation.

A handwritten schedule: his last season and the one he never saw.

Quarterbacks called their own plays; the coach made sure they knew the odds.

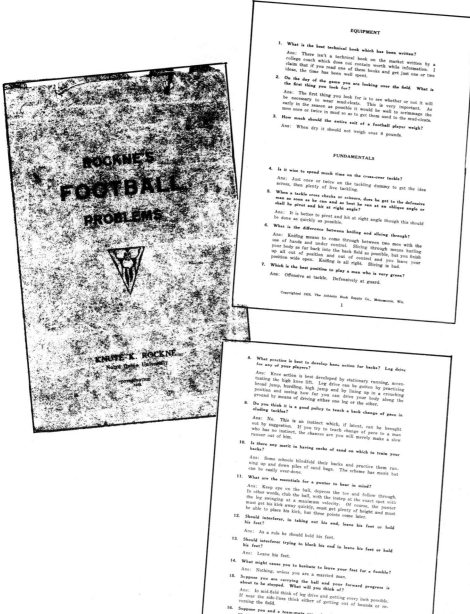

EQUIPMENT

1. **What is the best technical book which has been written?**

   Ans: There isn't a technical book on the market written by a college coach which does not contain worth while information. I claim that if you read one of these books and get just one or two ideas, the time has been well spent.

2. **On the day of the game you are looking over the field. What is the first thing you look for?**

   Ans: The first thing you look for is to see whether or not it will be necessary to wear mud-cleats. This is very important. As early in the season as possible it would be well to scrimmage the men once or twice in mud so as to get them used to the mud-cleats.

3. **How much should the entire suit of a football player weigh?**

   Ans: When dry it should not weigh over 8 pounds.

FUNDAMENTALS

4. **Is it wise to spend much time on the cross-over tackle?**

   Ans: Just once or twice on the tackling dummy to get the idea across, then plenty of live tackling.

5. **When a tackle cross checks or scissors, does he get to the defensive man as soon as he can and as best he can at an oblique angle or shall he pivot and hit at right angle?**

   Ans: It is better to pivot and hit at right angle though this should be done as quickly as possible.

6. **What is the difference between knifing and slicing through?**

   Ans: Knifing means to come through between two men with the use of hands and under control. Slicing through means hurling your body as far back into the back field as possible, but you finish up all out of position and out of control and you leave your position wide open. Knifing is all right. Slicing is bad.

7. **Which is the best position to play a man who is very green?**

   Ans: Offensive at tackle. Defensively at guard.

Copyrighted 1926, The Athletic Book Supply Co., Menomonie, Wis.

1

8. **What practice is best to develop knee action for backs? Leg drive for any of your players?**

   Ans: Knee action is best developed by stationary running, accentuating the high knee lift. Leg drive can be gotten by practicing broad jump, hurdling, high jump and by lining up in a crouching position and seeing how far you can drive your body along the ground by means of driving either one leg or the other.

9. **Do you think it is a good policy to teach a back change of pace in eluding tackles?**

   Ans: No. This is an instinct which, if latent, can be brought out by suggestion. If you try to teach change of pace to a man who has no instinct, the chances are you will merely make a slow runner out of him.

10. **Is there any merit in having sacks of sand on which to train your backs?**

   Ans: Some schools blindfold their backs and practice them running up and down piles of sand bags. The scheme has merit but can be easily over-done.

11. **What are the essentials for a punter to bear in mind?**

   Ans: Keep eye on the ball, depress the toe and follow through. In other words, club the ball, with the instep at the exact spot with the leg swinging at a maximum velocity. Of course, the punter must get his kick away quickly, must get plenty of height and must be able to place his kick, but these points come later.

12. **Should interferer, in taking out his end, leave his feet or hold his feet?**

   Ans: As a rule he should hold his feet.

13. **Should interferer trying to block his end in leave his feet or hold his feet?**

   Ans: Leave his feet.

14. **What might cause you to hesitate to leave your feet for a fumble?**

   Ans: Nothing, unless you are a married man.

15. **Suppose you are carrying the ball and your forward progress is about to be stopped. What will you think of?**

   Ans: In mid-field think of leg drive and getting every inch possible. If near the side-lines think either of getting out of bounds or reversing the field.

16. **Suppose you and a team-mate are going for a loose ball and so is an opponent; what do you do?**

   Ans: Block opponent so team-mate can get ball.

Copyrighted 1926, The Athletic Book Supply Co., Menomonie, Wis.

2

Mr. Knute Rockne, Director of Athletics,
Notre Dame University,
South Bend, Indiana

BD:H

The CHRISTY WALSH SYNDICATE
Newspaper Service
570 SEVENTH AVE. ~ NEW YORK

May 23rd, 1927

Hendrik van Loon

Babe Ruth

John J. McGraw

Nick Altrock

Frederick G. Lieb

Jack Kearns

Ray McNamaraCHI

Tyrus R. Cobb

Walter Johnson

Rogers Hornsby

Fielding H Yost

Knute Rockne

Glenn S. Warner

Tad Jones

Dear Mr. Rockne:

We had written to you on Saturday, May 21st, requesting you to send us your story "Campus Comment" No. 3. Evidently our letters had crossed each other for today Mr. Walsh has handed me your third article which will be for release on Saturday or Sunday, June 11th or 12th.

The next story we will need, will be No. 4 for release on Saturday or Sunday, June 18th or 19th. This story should be in our office not later than Tuesday morning June 14th.

The following schedule is for your convenience:

Story No.	Release Date	Due in our Office
#1	May 18th or 19th	We have story
#2	June 4th or 5th	We have story
#3	June 11th or 12th	Received today
#4	June 18th or 19th	June 14th
#5	June 25th or 26th	June 21st
#6	July 2nd or 3rd	June 28th

Thanking you, we are

Yours,

B. Dahlstrom

THE CHRISTY WALSH SYNDICATE.

Rock's newspaper columns were distributed by the Christy Walsh syndicate, a nationwide operation whose clients read like a veritable *Who's Who* of 1920's sports superstars.

Rockne's Football Problems show the coach at his Socratic best, posing loaded questions and offering razor-sharp answers.

His monogram, folded eight ways,
was tucked in a small envelope.

His 1928 Olympic tour made a trans-Atlantic trek to the Amsterdam games.

V.
A Hunk and a Horseman
1931-1940

Rockne died March 31, 1931, when a Fokker F-10 that was ferrying him to Hollywood crashed in a field near Emporia, Kansas. Notre Dame was about to learn how irreplaceable the Rock really was.

To begin with, the University fell prey to an old, established business practice: when in danger of making a decision, appoint a committee. To honor Rock, so the story went, the title of head coach was terminated. Instead, the team was to be handled by Senior Coach Hunk Anderson and Junior Coach Jack Chevigny. Jesse Harper was recalled from his Kansas ranch to take over as athletic director.

The difference between the Harper and the Rockne reigns in the director's office is most evident in the handling of money. Rock used to walk around with a breast pocket full of tickets, filling orders for people he met on the street. Saturday mornings he would slip the senior football manager $500 and say, "Take care of things." A couple bucks for the ticket-takers, a couple bucks for the traffic cops, Rockne never thought another thing about it. Harper demanded a strict accounting of every cent. "All of us managers," remembers one, "used to sit up half the night in the bathrooms — the priests switched off all the other lights at eleven — just trying to get our ledgers to come out right. Harper went over those things with a magnifying glass. You would've had to get a receipt from a pay toilet."

Not that Harper had a feeling for playing Scrooge. He was simply the successful businessman Rockne had never become. The administration needed a man like Harper; they intended to regulate the revenues a lot more closely than when Rockne had been in charge. More money would be siphoned off the athletic program; football scholarships were cut to twenty; recruiting was out: it was the school's first attempt at football de-emphasis.

Blunt, tough, profane, Hunk Anderson was not a de-emphasizing kind of guy. Though an exceptional line coach, he had more than his share of problems as head man. The senior coach-junior coach nonsense was soon forgotten, but many still considered Hunk a thumb in the dike, an emergency replacement who had no business being considered for a permanent position.

Hunk Anderson. Grantland Rice called him, "pound for pound the toughest man I have ever known."

Not the least of Hunk's critics was Athletic Director Harper, who instructed student managers to file daily reports on anything and everything Hunk was doing at practice. Such tactics hardly built respect for the Hunk Anderson regime.

Nor did the hiring of Chevigny, far from Hunk's first choice as an assistant. Chevigny was young and cocky. He disagreed openly with his boss, often coaching the players to do the opposite of what Hunk had told them, with predictably disastrous results on the field.

Maybe, as has always been written, Hunk Anderson was in over his head. His three year record of 16-9-2 seems to show it. Maybe, though, he just had the misfortune of being the man who followed Rockne.

★ ★ ★

Dan Hanley wanted a football scholarship very badly. He got out his best suit, the one reserved for funerals and weddings, brushed it, picked off the lint. He polished his Sunday shoes for an hour. He borrowed a silk tie from the high roller down the street; invested in a stiff, white collar; pulled out the good shirt he had been saving for a special occasion.

Hanley dressed himself solemnly, meticulously, like a matador preparing for the bull. He was arrayed like the successor to God when he appeared before University Vice-President, Father Mulcaire.

The wiry priest never let Hanley introduce himself. "You're dressed better than anybody on campus," Mulcaire snapped. "It's obvious you don't need a scholarship. You're wasting my time. Beat it."

Hanley slunk home, tore off his clothes,

aimlessly donned the ragged duds from the bottom drawer of his dresser. Why not? he thought, and reappeared in Mulcaire's office clad in this tattered outfit.

Again, the priest did all the talking. "Who do you think you are?" He was boiling. "Coming in here dressed like that? We don't need bums like you at Notre Dame. Get out!"

★ ★ ★

You can run but you cannot hide. Albert Feeney, an old teammate of Rockne's, had been out of football for a long time. When the Irish visited Bloomington, Indiana, in 1931, Al good-naturedly agreed to hold the chains along the sidelines.

Midway through the third quarter, someone kicked him in the face and broke his nose.

When Al left the game, he discovered his car had been stolen.

★ ★ ★

Norm Greeney's play on the gridiron must have warmed the very cockles of Hunk Anderson's heart. The 180-pound guard from Ohio had a style reminiscent of Anderson's own: he was a brawler and a scrapper who would stop at nothing short of brass knuckles to carry out his assignment.

Sometimes opponents complained — as Pittsburgh did in 1931 — that Greeney took liberties with the rules of sportsmanship. Pitt thought the one-man terrorist attack deserved some penalty yardage. The refs disagreed. Greeney roamed the field unfettered and the Irish won the 1931 meeting, 25-12. A few of Pitt's youngsters spent the day more concerned with Norm Greeney's whereabouts than with the final score.

Nordy Hoffman showed up for the 1932 East-West Shrine Game in mid-season form. The same could not be said for the man opposing him in the line. Nordy walked all over the out-of-shape tackle. Finally, the opponent held up his hand to stop the mismatch. "Listen, Hoffman," wheezed the Westerner, "we're playing *for* crippled people, not *to* cripple people."

★ ★ ★

It's not the kind of statistic you'll see printed boldface in a Notre Dame program, but the smallest crowd ever to ease into Notre Dame Stadium for an Irish game came to see a 62-0 roasting of Drake on October 15, 1932: 6,663 spectators.

Alabama used to have a traveling squad bigger than that.

★ ★ ★

The chickens of 1931 came home to roost in 1932. Pittsburgh's timid underclassmen had grown into hardened veterans. When Notre Dame came to play, those vets had one immediate objective: to get Norm Greeney out of the game, preferably on a stretcher.

The game began. The Panther lineman ignored their blocking assignments. Fists flying, they charged Greeney's spot in the Notre Dame line. The punching in pile-ups was vicious. Pitt was getting their revenge — so they thought. The object of their abuse was actually a guy named Jim Harris.

Harris and Greeney had switched sides of the line since the previous year, and since the Panthers didn't remember Greeney's face or numer, only his position, Harris was the one getting trampled.

Greeney was a silent partner . . .

. . . Harris got the business.

Apparently Greeney watched the proceedings with a sigh, and kept his mouth shut.

The stampede continued unchecked into the second quarter. By then Jim Harris had so many cleat marks down the front of his body he was beginning to look like a breakfast waffle. He couldn't take it any longer.

The Pitt quarterback was calling a play. Harris shouted, "Check!" (There were no huddles. This was the signal used by an offensive player who didn't hear the play as it was called from scrimmage.)

The quarterback repeated the count, but — "Check!" — again he was interrupted. This time he realized that it was a Notre Dame player who was checking signals.

There was a befuddled pause. It was all the time Jim Harris needed. He stood up. "Listen you idiots," he advised the Panther eleven, "I'm *Harris!* The guy you want is *Greeney!* He's right down there."

Look at it this way, Norman — it was nice while it lasted.

★ ★ ★

When the Haskell Indians rode into South Bend for their 1932 pow-wow with the Irish, representatives of fifteen different Indian tribes dotted their roster. The quarterback called the signals in Chinook.

He must have been the only Chinook on the squad.

Haskell got massacred, 73-0.

★　★　★

Ed Moran and Ed Kenefake reviewed the situation. The football team would be returning that night from a season-ending game with USC. The student body planned a large rally at the train station, the year's final tribute to the Irish.

It wasn't good enough for Moran and Kenefake to merely show up as part of the mob. They wanted to make their presence felt. But how? "Let's get a Trojan horse — a white horse — and lead it into the station," suggested Moran.

Kenefake agreed. But a survey of every stable and farm in South Bend turned up no white horse. Moran was always working the angles. "We'll just get any old horse and make him white ourselves."

"How?" asked his sidekick.

"Lime."

Lime was the apparent answer. A bay gelding was given a thorough powdering with the stuff until he looked like — if you had a vivid imagination — a Trojan horse.

Most of the crowd was already sardined inside the station that night when there was a commotion at one entrance. Led by two boys, a very skittish horse that looked like a large powdered-sugar confection pranced in. The crowd parted to give it room. Then the trouble began. The poor gelding's lime coating began to heat up, as lime coatings will. Soon, the horse was uncontrollable.

He reared. He bucked. He dragged the two Eds along like tin cans behind a newlywed's car. Then he spotted an exit, and burst through it full speed. Presumably the horse didn't stop until it hit the nearest lake. Moran and Kenefake had nothing to show for their evening but rope-burned hands.

Some horses just weren't meant to be a different color.

★　★　★

In the thirties, Notre Dame made sure its Catholic students strictly obeyed Church regulations. This caused an occasional problem. A fellow named O'Brien was the product of a religiously-mixed marriage. One Sunday he would attend mass; the following Sunday he would golf.

When the authorities called him in, O'Brien tried to explain. "I go one week for my dad, the

Catholic." said O'Brien. "The next week I fool around. That's for my mother, the Methodist."

O'Brien did not last long at Notre Dame.

★　★　★

The opening game of the 1933 season was a tie with Kansas, a contest played in pouring rain. Neither team could make any headway, and as the Notre Dame staff watched the ball squirt all over the field, someone advised Hunk Anderson, "We need resin in there."

"Resin?" Hunk said. "Where is he? Get him in there, get him in."

★　★　★

Hash markers appeared in 1933. Up to this time, a ball was put into play wherever it had been downed. If your star runner made the mistake of getting tackled two inches from the sidelines, that's where the ball was hiked on the next play. To say the least, it made for some weird offensive sets. It also made for conservative, down-the-middle football, because no team wanted to get hemmed in against the sidelines.

Keeping the ball within the hash marks made for a more exciting, sweeping, wide-open game. Every expert in the country confidently predicted that the use of hash marks would cause an offensive explosion; telephone number scores would be the order of the day.

Hunk Anderson's boys weren't listening. In 1933 they were whitewashed six games out of nine, chalking up a measly season total of thirty-two points. Notre Dame had not done so badly since 1888. By the end of the season, Hunk was out of a job.

★　★　★

Part of the problem with Hunk's last team was the quarterbacking. Four novices shared the position, and they tended to lose track of little things, like what down it was. After watching his boys unnecessarily turn over the ball too many times, Hunk ordered Co-Captain Hugh Devore to act as a backseat driver, and remind the quarterback of the down after each play.

★   ★   ★

Imagine you just lost your job. Nope, can't get another one. Just about everybody else is out of work too. Better hurry to the bank — oops, sorry, the bank has gone under. Your savings have disappeared.

Now imagine there's no such thing as welfare, no social security, no unemployment insurance, no foodstamps, no federally-subsidized housing, no government loans to individuals.

Think about this: How are you going to eat tonight, or pay next month's rent? Don't bother moving on. The whole world's in the same soup.

Welcome to the Depression.

That was about the state of things when Elmer Layden took over at Notre Dame. The lanky Iowan with an infectious Midwestern twang had been the fullback of Rockne's Four Horsemen, an association he certainly had cause to regret over the years. The newspapers never let him forget it, replaying the Four Horsemen theme deafeningly in almost every game account, every column that mentioned the Notre Dame coach. Innumerable sports page cartoons were printed with Layden on a horse, or leading a horse, or looking like a horse, the bigger-than-life spirit of Rockne grinning benignly in the background. To the newspapers of the day, Elmer Layden seemed to be always the pupil, never the master.

No, Hunk Anderson's boys didn't have trouble remembering their positions. The labels were for an instructional film.

To his players, Layden either came across as a fine gentleman or a cold fish. No pep-talker or glad-hander, he gave pre-game speeches that were basically strategy sessions; his halftime remarks concentrated on reactions and adjustments to the enemy attack. His defensively-oriented teams reflected his own quiet, conservative personality. Glamorous football stars simply did not develop under Elmer Layden; closely knit team players did.

By the time Layden took over at Notre Dame, there was a new boss in Washington as well — Franklin Delano Roosevelt. His New Deal was government by alphabetical permutation: SEC, TVA, CCC, FDIC, WPA, The NRA: "We Do Our Part." There were fireside chats and brain trusts, packing the Supreme Court and packing for Hyde Park.

America's bread basket became a dust bowl.

Bank holidays begat soup kitchens and five-day work weeks. Utah was toasted all over the nation when it became the thirty-sixth state to repeal Prohibition. Liquor was in again; bootleggers looked for another racket.

The Lindbergh baby was kidnapped. Mayor Cermak was shot in Chicago. Public Enemy Number One, John Dillinger, was betrayed by the Lady in Red. America's Top Cop, J. Edgar Hoover, became a public hero.

The Dionne quintuplets were born; all over America, women developed small back pains just thinking about it. Amelia Earhart and Wiley Post took to the air; Franco took Spain; new, inexpensive cameras had everybody taking snapshots.

Edward VIII quit his job, which happened to be King of England, so he could marry an American divorcee. Meanwhile, Benny Goodman began a long reign as the King of Swing, his subjects jitterbugging the years away.

The dirigible *Hindenburg* went down in Lakehurst, New Jersey. The swastika went up in the Rhineland. Stalin purged and Hitler frothed. Neville Chamberlain became history's all-time sucker.

On the wide silver screen (what theater didn't boast one?) *Snow White* awakened people to the idea that cartoons were not just kids' stuff. W. C. Fields sneered; Mae West leered; Clark Gable was romantic; the Marx Brothers frantic. *Gone With the Wind* swept the nation.

Radios were commonplace now. And they brought more than Amos 'n' Andy. They brought college football. Imagine the effect of live sports broadcasts on people who had been raised with a victrola at best. A twist of the dial might bring twenty or more games into the living room. Thus began a malady which even today rages through America at epidemic proportions: the armchair fan.

★ ★ ★

When Father John O'Hara became Notre Dame's President in 1934, he was determined to upgrade the school's scholastic ranking. Among other requirements, he decreed that any student holding a University job had to maintain a 77% grade-point average. The rub: at that time, every football scholarship included University employment. Football players were not notoriously bookish. A few of them would have their scholarships lopped off because of this rule. Rather than see his program crippled, Coach Elmer Layden decided to fight the 77% solution.

Layden instructed his assistants to draw up a roster of prominent and successful alumni whose final grade-point averages had been below 77%. This list, Layden knew, would clearly discredit Father O'Hara's overstressed scholasticism. Just the threat of publishing the list would bring the administration to its knees.

Layden was still congratulating himself on this impending triumph of common sense when, a few days later, he learned that he was on the roll of Notre Dame's underachievers. "You qualified easily," he was told. "Your grade-point average was — "

"Hold it!" squealed Elmer Layden.

The coaching staff forgot all about making up that list.

And Layden learned to live with a brighter breed of ballplayer.

★ ★ ★

Unfortunately, the 77% grade-point rule cost Notre Dame some of its most appealing characters. One fellow, a big lineman, just sneaked out of school before the cutoff went into effect. He was a favorite of ours. During one gray practice, this beefy ballplayer gazed into the clouds.

"I tink," he mused, "it's gonna grizzle."

★ ★ ★

Jack Robinson: his assets were stable.

Jack Robinson, a center on the 1932 and 1934 squads, had money, and plenty of it. Enough money to own, among other things, a string of racehorses. Yessir, while his classmates were curled up with a penny dreadful, Jack was poring over *The Daily Racing Form*. While they were getting their shoes resoled he was trying to find a decent blacksmith. Depression? Did somebody say Depression?

The finest of Robinson's stable actually ran in the 1932 Kentucky Derby. The steed, a bay colt named Lucky Tom, took a leisurely spin around the Churchill Downs oval and finished "somewhere around twelfth" according to the next day's newspaper accounts. Lucky Tom, a betrayer of his thoroughbred ancestry, would have felt more at home pulling an ice wagon.

Owner Robinson saw the results pragmatically: "It was a very nice experience for Lucky Tom — socially, I mean. He met some very good horses."

★ ★ ★

The surest pledge of a deathless name
Is the silent homage of thoughts unspoken.
— *Henry Wadsworth Longfellow*

Assistant football coach Jake Kline drew up the roster of incoming freshman football players. On the opening day of practice, the team would arrange itself in a straight line, and Jake would walk along taking names. It was a hot and annoying ritual that both Jake and the boys disliked. No time for fooling around.

"Your name?" Jake asked a prospect from Staten Island.

"Shakespeare. William Shakespeare."

"Yeah," said Jake. He made a mental note to put the guy on the fourth team.

"Next." Jake pointed to the fellow beside Shakespeare.

"Longfellow," said the freshman.

"Oh," Jake replied. "Henry?"

"John."

"Yeah," drawled Jake. He scowled at Longfellow and Shakespeare. "Sure, those are your names."

These guys, he told himself, play when the Pope moves to Nebraska.

Of course, Shakespeare and Longfellow *were* their real names. ("They were in the doghouse till I found out for sure," growls Jake.) And they turned out to be pretty good ballplayers, as well as sporting names public relations men pray for.

★ ★ ★

Pity poor Shakespeare, who endured countless atrocious puns on his name. He barely cracked the starting line-up before he was tabbed "The Bard of Staten Island." Rumors spread that he was flunking out of Notre Dame because he could not pass English. After Bill's heroics in the Ohio State game, teammate Wayne Millner noted, "Shakespeare will never get credit for this. Someone's sure to say Roger Bacon did it."

If this sort of talk bothered Shakespeare, he must have taken it out on the ball. A punter extraordinaire, he still holds the Notre Dame record with an 86-yard boot against Navy in 1935.

★ ★ ★

The players sat in a nervous circle and stared at the floor. Sure, they were only the B Team playing at Niagara in a game no one would ever care about. Still, they were from Notre Dame. For many, it was their first game for Coach Jake Kline. The players wondered what kind of pep talk he would give. They had gone to Notre Dame with visions of a Rockne-like coach urging them forward in stentorian tones. What would Kline say? Perhaps a speech that rhythmically built to a climax of GO! FIGHT! WIN! Perhaps a sharp harangue, demeaning the team's ability and thus urging them on to greater victory. Maybe a clipped strategy

session, leaving the emotions to bubble and burst with the opening kickoff.

The players waited.

The door opened. Coach Jake Kline stuck his head in. "Okay," he said, "everybody take that last nervous piss and get out there.'

★ ★ ★

A few years later, the word was out on Jake. during a B game in Miami, as Notre Dame took the field to start the second half, Jake was approached by an opposing coach.

"Give 'em a big pep talk?" asked the Miami mentor.

"Naw," Jake admitted. "I couldn't get a word in. They were all listening to the Army-Notre Dame game on the radio."

★ ★ ★

Moose Krause was selected to play in the first College All-Star Football Game in 1934. The All-Stars were to meet the Chicago Bears, who had taken the 1934 NFL Championship largely on the bountiful talents of Fullback Bronko Nagurski. Bronko shed tacklers the way a dog shakes off water. At top speed, he was tougher to stop than *The Panama Limited*. Moose — lucky fellow — was given the task of defensing him.

He was to line up on the same side of the field as Bronko and attempt to keep the fullback from gathering steam on an end run. Krause soon learned that he wasn't the only player keeping track of Bronko.

George Musso, a Bear lineman, assumed his stance for the game's first play from scrimmage. "Hey Moose," he hissed across the line, "I just come outta da huddle."

"I can see that." Krause didn't sense the point of such obvious information.

"What I learned in da huddle is dat Bronko is gonna be runnin' right through here."

"What are you telling me for?"

Musso frowned impatiently, "I don't know what *you* got planned. But when Bronko comes this way, *I'm* gettin' outta his path."

★   ★   ★

Jim McKenna hollered out the signals, then caught the center snap and back-pedalled into the intricate weave of an Ohio State spinner play. But his teammates in the prep team backfield, lacking a sense of timing or direction or both, tangled awkwardly, and McKenna was nearly decapitated when the varsity defense zeroed in on him. His head whiplashed onto the Cartier Field turf. Constellations whirled; his knees betrayed him when he tried to stand. A cadre of student managers scurried out and assisted him to the sidelines. After a once-over by the trainer, McKenna was escorted to the infirmary for observation. Meanwhile, the coaches had requisitioned another cannon fodder quarterback and sent him to his fate.

That's the way it is with prep teamers the week before a big game. Pain becomes an intimate acquaintance. And as big games go, the Ohio State game of 1935 was one of the king-hellers of all time. Both the Irish and the Buckeyes were undefeated. A number-one ranking was in the balance. Head coaches were a study in contrasts: even-tempered Elmer Layden against Francis "Bar the Gates of Mercy" Schmidt; Layden's methodical attack against Schmidt's razzle-dazzle spinner offense that revved instantly into overdrive and never looked back.

The game lived up to every bit of its advance billing, and then some. Notre Dame's incredible 18-13 win has been called the Game of the Century, and few of the 81,000 who saw the mind-boggling battle would dispute that label. They stood in Buckeye Stadium, unmoving, for thirty minutes after the final gun, trying to fathom what they had seen. Sportswriters found no adjective adequate to describe the frantic finish.

But we digress. Back to Jim McKenna. The scrawny backliner from St. Paul, Minnesota, had not been seriously hurt. He was back at practice the day after the mugging. And on Friday, even though he wasn't on the traveling squad, McKenna decided he'd accompany the team to Columbus. After all, he had practically fractured his skull for the cause.

The senior sub didn't have money to make the trip, or a ticket to the game, but that was okay. To get to Columbus he skived — stowed away — on the team train. Skiving was strictly forbidden by Notre Dame and the railway companies; so naturally, football trains carried contraband students in every nook and cranny. Aided by a couple of teammates, McKenna hid in a berth for the passage.

There remained the problem of acquiring a ticket. McKenna had planned to find a generous scalper, but the market was bullish; Saturday morning scalpers were getting fifty dollars and up for a single ducat. Security around the stadium was tight, so gate-crashing was out. As a last resort he dashed to the Irish dressing room, hoping to get a sideline pass.

Luckily, a student manager — the same one who had taken him to the infirmary — was guarding the door, and McKenna was admitted. Inside, he mingled jovially with the players, most of whom were surprised to see him. Then a voice caused the visitor to cringe: "What do you think you're doing here?" Elmer Layden was surprised to see him too.

Stammering, McKenna tried to explain his plight, but Layden cut him short, "Well, as long as you're here, you might as well dress. Get a uniform."

The kid from St. Paul donned the uniform, minus pads — why carry armor on non-combat duty? — and took the field with the Irish. He found a good vantage point on the bench and parked there to watch the Game of the Century. Or at least to watch most of it.

Late in the final stanza, with Ohio State desperately protecting a 13-12 lead, the Irish recovered a fumble at midfield. With less than a minute on the timer, Pilney bulled to the OSU 19 on a busted play. Layden, forbidden by the rule book from signalling a play from the sidelines, sent in a quarterback with a play. The pass failed. Forty seconds in the game.

The team looked to Layden, expecting another directive. But because of a substitution rule under which a player could not re-enter a game in the quarter, the coach was out of signal-callers. Unless . . . his eye caught a padless figure at the end of the bench — Jim McKenna! The startled prepper was summoned. Layden gave him the signals to call. He was shoved onto the field.

McKenna was brilliant. He rattled off the numbers and, as the Buckeye defense pressed furiously, chopped down a lineman. From his knees, he watched Wayne Millner grab Bill Shakespeare's TD toss. 18-13, Notre Dame!

Not bad, Jim McKenna. For a guy who wasn't supposed to be in the train, the stadium, a uniform, or the game — not bad at all.

★   ★   ★

The best story about the OSU game concerns a hopelessly drunk Buckeye fan who was seen toddling down High Street after Notre Dame's stunning victory.

"What about the game?" the drunk was asked.

"The firsht three quarters are great," hiccupped the high Ohioan, "but don't bother staying for the fourth."

★ ★ ★

Elmer Layden, after looking over the statistics for the 1935 season: "The fumble was our best play."

★ ★ ★

Elmer Layden, in another of those preposterous ploys that coaches love so well, broke out the yarn and knitting needles when his boys were playing like women.

Every two years, the Irish travel to Los Angeles for the Southern Cal game. Every two years, Hollywood casts its magic spell on the impressionable college kids from South Bend. In the 1930's, the movie capital was enjoying its Golden Age, and Hollywood's blend of fantasy and reality was especially beguiling.

"We were dead-end kids," remembers an old benchwarmer. "Most of us were from the East or Midwest, where life could be pretty grim. All of a sudden, we were out where you could pick oranges right off the trees. We could swim in the ocean or climb a mountain, and most of us hadn't seen an ocean or a mountain in our lives. And, of course, we got to meet the movie stars.

"The movie people were as interested in us as we were in them. I mean, we were *Notre Dame!* But you try meeting Bing Crosby and Bob Hope. It gets so you don't want to go home."

A case in point: After one Irish-Trojan contest, most of the team was invited to an opulant Beverly Hills mansion. Food and drink were spread for a feast. Pin-up girl Betty Grable was fox-trotting her million-dollar legs across the dance floor. Other Hollywood stars wandered about, signing autographs, sipping drinks, slipping in and out of character. And each ballplayer had a special escort, a pretty girl from the movies.

It was an incredibly heady experience for young fellows from a small Catholic school in the Midwest. Some men handled it better than others. Bob Douglas (the name has been changed to protect a happily married man) did not handle it well at all.

Without meaning to shatter anyone's illusions, the authors must point out that not all Notre Damers play with "a strength the strength of ten because their hearts are pure." Bob was one of those who rated a pure heart a poor second to having a good time, especially with football season out of the way.

At this party, Bob attached himself immediately to the bar. Following the advice of Alexander Pope — "Drink deep or taste not!" — Bob quickly sloshed down enough alcohol to burn the finish off a dining room table. Then he disappeared.

After hours of partying, the players bid good-bye to glamour and hurried to the train station for the return trip to Notre Dame. Someone noticed that Bob was missing. ("It was too quiet," the player remembers.) A hardy group of volunteers doubled back to the mansion and began a room-to-room search. They finally found the party boy upstairs. Bob was a bit under the influence. He was hiding under a bed.

The team captain, a respected leader, peered under the springs. "We really ought to go, Bob," he cooed.

"Noooo," moaned Bob. "I'm never going back." He got a good strong grip on the bedpost.

A policeman was called in.

"Our train leaves any minute," hissed the captain.

The cop nodded. He had been trained to handle emergencies just like this. He stretched himself out on the floor, propped his head up with his hands, and began talking to Bob. Soon the two were babbling like old lodge buddies.

"I hate to ask you to leave," the policeman finally dredged up the dreaded subject, "but the guy who uses this room says he has trouble getting to sleep when there's someone hiding under the bed. You understand. Why don't you come out? We're all friends here."

"Well," said Bob.

"Yes?" said the policeman.

"Well," said Bob, "I'll come out on one condition."

"Yes?"

"You gotta ride me around the block on your motorcycle."

The policeman was used to Hollywood parties. He agreed without blinking an eye.

In a matter of minutes, the cop had whisked Bob through the sun-baked streets of Los Angeles and deposited him not back at the mansion, but in front of the train station. Under the kind direction of his teammates, Bob lurched to his platform. An Eastbound train was steaming up, and through that steam, Bob saw cloudy visions of South Bend: the rain and snow and leaden skies; the wind and cold and everlasting chill; steam heat, bad food, football practice, classwork.

Bob reeled. It was more than he could bear.

I'll climb a palm tree, he decided, and wait out the winter. Bob eyed the platform. There were no palm trees. A lesser man might have tossed in the towel right there, but not Bob. Undaunted, he bolted from his teammates and tumbled into a stairwell, where he wrapped his arms and legs tightly around an iron railing and held on with all the power his impure heart could muster.

The team captain summoned the team managers.

"We got him to the station," said the captain. "It's your job to get him on the train."

"All aboard," crowed the conductor.

The team managers threw nervous looks at each other. Notre Dame had never before had a roster name stamped, "Missing: Lost in Transit." The managers scrambled for whatever weapons they could find.

"Last call," bleated the train man. "All aboard."

Notre Dame's managers attacked. Armed with buckets of ice water, they doused Bob and pried him loose. Bob fought it. He swung and kicked and begged to be left behind.

"Take her out," cried the conductor to the engineer. The train rumbled and stumbled and began to roll.

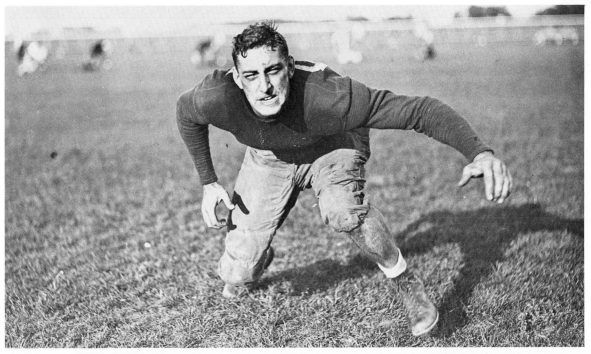

EEEAAGHHH!
How would you like to dig in against this guy? It's Butch Pfefferle, who played every game in a shoulder harness. We would suggest a muzzle.

No one works faster than a group of poor student managers about to lose their only ride home. Bob was carried, still struggling, alongside the moving train. A door opened. Bob was tossed in. The managers followed.

"Somebody had to sit on that guy till we reached Utah," remembers a teammate.

Cal-li-for-nya, there he goes.

★   ★   ★

Bill Steinkemper was a strong guard and a smart one. But during the Pitt game of 1936, he was trapped into the backfield, blindsided, crushed, and finally sat upon by a mammoth end. There lay Steinkemper with outstretched but useless arms as two pulling guards ran by. Two halfbacks streaked around, then the fullback, and finally the ball-carrying quarterback.

Steinkemper watched it all.

There was nothing else he could do.

He sang:

"I . . . love a parade."

★   ★   ★

Some statistics from the 1936 game against the University of Southern California:

ND		USC
19	first downs	1*
137	yards gained passing	18
274	yards gained rushing	31
411	total yards	49

*First down gained on penalty.

Final Score: Notre Dame 13, USC 13.

★   ★   ★

Captain John Lautar was knocked cold before the 1936 Army game. No, not by some strong-arm gambler who had bet the family shirt on the Cadets. Not even by the Army mule. Lautar knocked himself out.

He was excitedly leading the team down a dark runway to the dugout when he met a low-hanging girder. His teammates had to step over him, one by one, to get to the field.

After this, Lautar went nowhere without his helmet.

★   ★   ★

So much for dangers to the unhelmeted head. Bill Buckley insisted on playing football barefoot. Not one of those beach-bum punters or Hawaiian field-goal kickers, Buckley was simply a halfback who enjoyed wiggling his toes in the cooling grasses of autumn. Since faces, let alone feet, are often cleated during football practice, you would have to say that Buckley was taking an awful chance for one of life's little pleasures. Occasionally, a coach could prevail upon him to slip into some shoes before scrimmaging, but after a few plays the cleats would come sailing back to the sidelines, and Buckley would be barefoot again.

You have to admire a guy who knows what he likes. Must be why he never logged even one minute of playing time.

★   ★   ★

For the youngsters who grew up in the insecure lap of the Depression a chance to participate in high school sports was a luxury, like a belly full of food or an extra pair of shoes. An athletic scholarship to college? That was a dream hardly worth dreaming. More likely a boy out of high school found himself shoveling coal, loading freight cars or stacking lumber for a dollar a day. The lucky ones like Chuck Sweeney, who parlayed their talent for football into a college education, have never forgotten.

We met Chuck Sweeney, a white-haired gentleman with a sparkling smile and a crippling handshake, in an office in Notre Dame's supply warehouse on the northern edge of the campus. Sweeney has taken a post-retirement job there, supervising the flow of soft drinks, paper towels, light bulbs and other disposables to campus buildings. It keeps him busy and, judging by his still-muscular build, keeps him fit.

We had seen it written that he became a first team All-America end in 1937 without catching a pass in his career. Interesting. True?

Sweeney smiled an easy smile when we asked. Asked about their college careers, some men, in the effort to recollect, screwed up their faces as if we were drilling for bone marrow. But Chuck Sweeney just smiled. Quite obviously, he had heard this tale before. "Nah, that's not true," he snorted. "I'm not sure how that got started. Actually I caught six or seven passes — not a lot, but we stayed mostly on the ground back then."

We asked if he would hazard a guess on the source of the fabrication.

"You know," he remarked, "I've always suspected Charlie Callahan was at the bottom of it. My strong suit was defense, and I guess that story was supposed to draw attention to my defensive play. It didn't pop up until a long time after I had graduated. Now, people read that Chuck Sweeney was an All-American end who never caught a pass and they're supposed to think, 'Hey, old Chuck must've been good on defense.' Yep — sounds like something Charlie would think up." (Callahan, for many years the Notre Dame Sports Information Director, would have invented a story about his grandmother if he thought it would get her invited to the Hula Bowl.)

There it was, an interesting story shot to hell when truth so rudely broke in. But Sweeney continued to reminisce.

"When we were on a road trip, not all of the players would get a berth on the train," he said. "Some of the guys — the guys who didn't figure to play much — would have to sleep in a seat. So what we'd do is find a fella who was making his first trip with the team. We'd tell him that he didn't have to stay in his seat all night, that he was splitting a berth with a teammate. We'd give him the number of the berth he was sharing and tell him to rouse his partner at two in the morning, when it was time to switch places. 'Course," — here the big smile broke out — "his 'partner' was a regular passenger who had no idea that someone would be climbing into his bed at two in the morning."

It sounded like a scene hatched by the Marx Brothers.

"Oh, it could get funny, let me tell you," he said. "Especially when the kid wouldn't catch on right away. The passenger would kick, and the kid would think, 'I'll be damned if anyone on this team's gonna keep me outta *my* bunk!' and try to yank the fellow out by the leg."

The vision is comical — an indignant sophomore tugging the leg of a slightly-hysterical anvil salesman from Altoona. We resist the great temptation to ask Mr. Sweeney if he was ever the sophomore.

For a while longer, we banter. But before we leave, Chuck Sweeney has one thing to tell us. As he spoke he leaned forward at this desk, and for the first time in the afternoon, the big smile melted completely away.

"You know, when I was a kid down in Bloomington, Illinois, there was never any money around — for anything. Not that we were poor by 1930's standards; but we were sure poor by today's standards. We didn't have the choices that today's kids have. As soon as you were old enough you got a job to supplement the family income, and that, " — he rapped his knuckles on the desk for emphasis — was that. "

"The five boys in our family all slept in a cramped little room. All the heat in the house came from a woodburning stove, so there was never enough heat in winter. And with our appetites there wasn't enough food, ever. I can remember always being hungry. Sometimes my high school football coach could spare me the money to buy lunch, but otherwise I went without it." He leaned back and gave a barely-perceptible shake of the head. For an instant it appeared he would laugh. The idea of not having food to eat was as ludicrous as a pink little salesman getting toppled from his berth on a train. But the instant passed.

"My high school coach had sort of taken me under his wing, convinced my parents that I had a chance to get a ride to college for my football playing. I don't think I ever believed it. I know for sure I didn't believe it when our parish priest told me I could get a ride to Notre Dame. People like me just didn't go to Notre Dame!

"I remember this: when I got to South Bend I had seven dollars in my pocket, and no clothes but the ones I had on my back. But for the first time in my life I had three meals a day and a room that was warm in the winter. And they were giving me a college education in exchange for my football playing. What could've been better? I can tell you for certain there wasn't anyplace in the world I would've rather been. Notre Dame was a . . . a *haven* to me." Sweeney sat back, the story over.

What do you bring away from a Depression? The cold? The hunger? The cardboard in your shoes or the patches in your dungarees?

If you're Chuck Sweeney you bring away a clear sense of the debts you owe. And you owe deeply to Notre Dame.

★ ★ ★

Chuck Sweeney today.

Time-out, Irish. Scrap Iron Young, the excitable Notre Dame trainer, bustled onto the field to treat an injured player. While applying some tape to the injury (taping injuries and rubbing them were the staples of Scrap Iron's technique), he noticed another player hurt, this one more seriously.

Joe Zwers, the Irish captain, had taken a nasty poke and was stumbling back to the huddle, bowed at the waist, hands over his face. "Joe!" barked the trainer. "Joe, where is it you're hurt?"

Motts Tonelli at Notre Dame.

"My nose," was the muffled reply.

"Joe," said Scrap Iron, noting the prominence of Zwers' proboscis, "you've got to be more specific."

★ ★ ★

Just a thought . . . the red-headed Zwers must hold the most unassailable niche in the Notre Dame record book: last place on the all-time roster.

★ ★ ★

Motts Tonelli, Notre Dame fullback from 1936 to 1938, does not revel in it. He's not even sure when the war started. "Let me see . . .," he mutters. "December?" Tilting his head back, he lets his eyes cloud. He is trying to remember something he has every right to forget. "That's it." He brings his eyes level with yours. "December it started."

What Tonelli is talking about is World War II. In the spring of 1942, Tonelli was stationed with the United States Army on the Bataan Peninsula of the Philippine Islands. Now, in the *National Geographic Magazine,* Bataan may look like some sort of primitive paradise. In reality it is a steaming maelstrom of mountain, jungle and swamp. Bataan simply defies human existence, but never so much as in the spring of 1942.

At that time, the Imperial Japanese Army was attacking from the North. The Americans, boxed into a trap of their own making, were slowly starving to death. For the soldiers, there was a half-ration of rice a day. The horses had already been cooked and eaten. Some people were trying monkey stew.

On Good Friday, April 3, 1942, Japanese General Homma began a new offensive. Debilitated by hunger and disease, facing certain slaughter, the Americans surrendered on April 9.

This was followed by one of the most infamous episodes of the Pacific War. American and Philippine prisoners were forced to march out of Bataan — a distance of almost one hundred miles — without food or water. The prisoners were beaten and clubbed to hurry their step. Stragglers, those who could go no further, were bayonetted or shot. This savagery lasted a full seven days. It was called The Bataan Death March, and Motts Tonelli walked every inch of it.

"There weren't too many roads into Bataan," says Tonelli. "So they wanted us out of there and off their supply lines in a hurry. They wanted to get their guys in.

"And it was rough. I remember at night, when we would be pushed over to the side of the road to sleep. I would spread my shirt in the grass to catch the dew. Next morning, I'd hold the shirt above my mouth, and I'd wring out the shirt and try to catch drops of water on my tongue. When it didn't work, I'd suck on the shirt for some moisture.

"It's not easy to explain — it's harder for others to understand — but I think my Notre Dame football experience helped me on the march. The hard work, the discipline. Getting my mind set to sacrifice for one goal. Of course my goal then was just to stay alive."

Tonelli lived through the Death March, and spent the next three-and-a-half years in a Japanese prison camp. Again, he credits his experience at Notre Dame with helping him to survive.

"I would lay there at night," he remembers, "and I'd think a lot about Notre Dame. I'd think about the grotto, and my professors, and people who meant something to me there. I'd pray, and Notre Dame would come back to me. It got me through . . well, it got me through an awful lot."

Tonelli works in an air-conditioned office now. He stays in shape. He has lunch with friends, and at night he goes home to his family.

On his desk is a small American flag; scattered across his office, the usual Fighting Irish knick-knacks and souvenirs. That's all, for what he and hundreds like him learned cannot be engraved on a plaque or stuck in a record book. Wisdom, courage, hope: big words; words we easily, cynically dismiss. But more than words to Motts Tonelli. Thanks, in part, to Notre Dame.

★ ★ ★

Motts Tonelli, POW.

Fans of the winning team in the annual Notre Dame-Army confrontation were so persistent in storming the field and, in the post-game euphoria of victory, dismantling the Yankee Stadium goalposts, that Colonel Jake Rupert, the stadium's owner, decided to take preventive action. He installed "disappearing goalposts." As the final gun sounded, field attendants scuttled out, collapsed the uprights mechanically, and slid them into holes in the ground.

Shhh! Don't disturb the Colonel. He's in his laboratory, perfecting his latest invention: disappearing referees.

★ ★ ★

Will Rogers was on campus for the day and Burnie Bauer, campus politico and walk-on footballer, was assigned to give him a guided tour. The pair strolled along, Rogers commenting in his homespun fashion about anything that caught his fancy.

The cowboy philosopher allowed as how Notre Dame's springtime greenery sure differed from his own Oklahoma sod. "And you know, Burnie," he remarked to his guide, "I'm partly responsible for that."

Bauer wanted to know how.

"Well sir, every time I ride an airplane out of Chicago, I get this callin' about the time we reach South Bend. So I just lean out over Notre Dame and answer Mother Nature."

★ ★ ★

NOTRE DAME

Will Rogers (l.) obviously likes Elmer Layden.

On the opening kickoff of the 1937 Army game, Bunny McCormick suffered a vicious block and lost four teeth. While Bunny was watching twenty years of steady brushing go to waste, the wobbly kickoff sailed untouched, out of bounds. So the ball was never in play, the clock didn't start, and the whole thing had to be done over.

This means that Bunny lost his bridgework in a play that never was in a game that hadn't started.

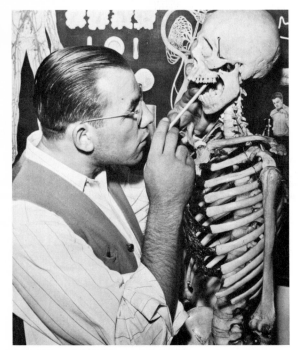

Milt Piepul (1940 captain): Where were you when Bunny McCormick needed you?

★ ★ ★

The team was down, the Irish were losing. As the players limped into the locker room at halftime, they helped themselves to the sugar cubes, orange and lemon slices that were laid out for them.

Elmer Layden had nothing. He was preparing himself. And when he was ready, he gathered his team in front of the two rows of lockers. The players swallowed their sugar and threw down their lemon wedges. They sat and looked up. They knew what was coming.

Layden was attempting a rare emotional halftime speech. Success or defeat could depend on just this: Elmer Layden's ability to stir up a team. He spoke a sentence and paused dramatically. Right away, a strange tinkling noise was heard. Layden began again. Again, there it was: clink, clink, tinkle, clink. Layden tried once more. Once more he paused for dramatic effect, only to have it blotted out by that weird tinkling sound.

Visibly disturbed, Coach Layden listened for the sound, located it, and stormed behind the lockers in the back of the room. There was reserve quarterback Butch Bruno, crouching in a litter of lemon peels and ground sugar cubes. Butch thrust a glass of discolored liquid toward the angered Layden.

"Look, Coach," said Butch proudly. "Lemonade!"

★ ★ ★

For all you devotees of bird-calling:

"Aaagghh! What? You lousy half-witted one-eyed bum! Ahhh, no. Come on!"

We all recognize that as the mating call of the big time I've-seen-better-referees-in-a-circus-sideshow college coach. Sometimes the song has a bit more brine to it, but the general characteristics are always the same: a sudden, sharp mournful warble; a brief interrogative chirp followed by an ornate descriptive phrase; a delicate romantic denial; a final haunting exhoration uttered with melancholy throatiness.

"Chjees! Can you believe that? We're lucky on that one, boys. Okay, okay, let's go get 'em."

★ ★ ★

Yes, it's the song of the rare he-made-a-mistake-but-we'll-take-it mentor. The call is divided in two. The first is hissed under the breath and toward the bench whilst the coach preens himself slightly. The second is a cheery trill blasted across the field and often accompanied by a rump slap, provided there is a player or assistant coach within patting distance.

Both of these calls were most vividly recorded during the 1938 Notre Dame-Carnegie Tech meeting. Undefeated Tech was driving for a score in the second half of a scoreless tie. Everybody in the stadium knew it was fourth down except Paul Getchell. Normally, Getchell's opinion would not hold much sway, but for this game he was the referee.

"Third down," he told the Scotties' quarterback.

"Are you sure it's not fourth?"

"Third down." The voice of authority.

To his credit, the Tech quarterback refused to argue. Gifts like this are infrequent and should not be questioned too severely.

Tech sent a short running play up the middle, not enough for a first down. Then Mr. Getchell noticed his error and awarded the ball to Notre Dame on downs. This evoked the two ear-piercing calls described above.

Getchell appealed to Elmer Layden, who rightly refused to give up the ball. Getchell appealed to Carnegie Tech Coach Bill Kern, who rightly argued that his team had been tricked. After a cacophony of hooting and screeching, the flap ended with

1938's "S-Men": (from bottom) Ben Sheridan, Harry Stevenson, Steve Sitko, and Bob Saggau.

Notre Dame in possession. The Irish promptly moved downfield for the game's only score.

A footnote: Carnegie Tech shared the Sugar Bowl that year with Texas Christian University and graciously invited Getchell to umpire the contest, a delightful bit of sportsmanship that backfired badly.

The deviously clever TCU attack used Getchell as target and interference. Horned Toad receivers simply junked their patterns and followed Getchell wherever he might go; the quarterback always lifted his passes toward the unfortunate umpire. Getchell couldn't help it: he was messed up in pass plays all afternoon, unwillingly screening the wiley TCU receivers. Carnegie Tech lost another game. Getchell seemed to blame. What Coach Bill Kern said during this one has, mercifully, not been recorded.

After the debacle, Getchell was invited to dine with about fifteen other people at a fine New Orleans night spot. Midway through the meal the host rose, collected several doggy bags of food, and slipped out the side door. Getchell was stuck with the bill.

★ ★ ★

Notre Dame won the 1939 Carnegie Tech game by a nose. John McIntyre's to be exact. He thrust it between a Tech place kick and the crossbar, blocking the boot and preserving the 7-6 victory.

★ ★ ★

On February 3, 1941, Elmer Layden resigned his post at Notre Dame to become the first commissioner of the National Football League. No one tried to talk him out of leaving.

"I still think," says Father John Cavanaugh,

Every coach's dream: heft in the backfield. That's Kate Smith joining the 1940 backs.

Notre Dame's ex-president, "that Layden was the best athletic director we ever had." To be sure, the Thin Man had a knack for keeping the old rivalries bubbling while attracting fresh, famous opponents. Even those old Big Ten snobs, Michigan and Ohio State, climbed aboard at his request. The suicide schedules brought the University money, prestige, but not national championships, no undefeated seasons. It's hard to imagine that the fans expected more from Layden than his 47-13-3 record, but they did. Looking back to the months of confusion following Rockne's death, the good-natured but inadequate tenure of Hunk Anderson, the conclusion is that Elmer Layden left the woodpile a good deal higher than he found it.

★ ★ ★

VI.

Irish Football Nicknames

There's no one named Dutch or Lefty here. This is top-drawer material, the *elite* file: the very best in Notre Dame football nicknames.

Ghost Casper
Moon Mullins
Porky McGill
Popeye Costa

Sweet Pea Daberio
Beano Neece
Chile Walsh
Pepper O'Donnell
Taco Alvarado
Peaches Nadolney
Cornie Clatt
Pickles Winsouer
Goofy Nuts Lynch

Snake Hips Maher
Squint-Eye O'Keefe
Spearhead Wendell

Turk Oaas
Buck Shaw
Lank Smith
Rollo Stein

Harpo Gladieux
Betty Grable

Fay Wood
Rosey Dolan
Cupid Glynn
Smoush Donovan
Smousherette Donovan

Waltzin' Willie Whightkin
Scooter Coutre
Slip Madigan
Clipper Smith

Scrap Iron Young
Zipper Lathrop
Gold Coast Billy Ryan

Pole DeNardo
Barn Seiler
Tree Adams
Fod Cotton

Deacon Jones
Sonny Church

Shorty Longman
Fuzzy McGlew
Mugsy McGrath
Paddy Cohen
Happy Lonergar
Rangy Miles
Dippy Evans

Goose Gander
Birdie Keller
Ducky Holmes
Stork McCullum
Chick Maggioli

Hornet Bake
Squeeter Conway
Cocky Roach

Foot Ruell
Calves Reynolds
Thumb Piepul
Jaw O'Brien
Head O'Marra
Pudge Puntillo

Cap Edwards
Bootie Albert
Bubba Galanis
Buddah Norri

Duke Millheam
King Farley
Judge Carberry

Hoot King
Pertoot Healy
Jepers Cullinan
Copper Lynch
Sniper Seis

Dinger McCabe
Dinny Shea

Bump Harshman
Rip Miller
Slug McGannon

Big Buster Costa
Smasher Corollo
Bumper Waldorf
Boom-Boom Schulz
Thunder Flanigan
Crash Dubesec

Rock Bowers
Rocky Bleier

Hunk Anderson
Brick Belden

Red Hering
Red Salmon

Dog Nicola
Black Dog Signaigo
Bulldog Ecuyer
Kitty Gorman

Horse Mehre
Bronko Nagurski (Jr.)
Bunny McCormick
Rabbit Ward
Moose Krause
Tiger McGrath
Gator Zloch
Turtle Roy
Bull Budynkiewicz

Blue Mundee

Wayne the Train Bullock
Perfect Play Flanigan
One Play O'Brien
Old Unreliable Oracko
Chi Chi Ciechanowicz

Bye-Bye Bliey

VII.
Almost a Religion
1941-1953

The guru strikes an inscrutable pose.

On the same day that Elmer Layden resigned at Notre Dame, Frank Leahy was sitting in an office six hundred miles away and putting his name on a contract that made him the coach of the Boston College Eagles for the next five years. Leahy had insisted on an alma mater clause. He was going to need it. Within two weeks he was in South Bend, inking yet another pact, this one naming him the head football coach and athletic director of the University of Notre Dame.

For Francis William Leahy, it was a dream come true.

He was as colorful a character as ever stalked the sidelines. Hailing from the harsh frontier town of Winner, South Dakota, he served on the lines of Rockne's last and finest teams until a knee injury ended his playing days. His senior year found him constantly at Rockne's side, an unofficial student coach learning from the master. It was as if Rockne had reached out and picked his successor — a theme the newspapers drove heavily home when Leahy arrived to lead the Irish.

Handsome in a sad-eyed sort of way, Leahy talked like the hero of a nineteenth century romance, his language stilted and dignified. He called his players "lads;" football helmets were "bonnets;" Everyone was addressed by his full Christian name: not John or Johnny, but Jonathan Lujack.

An almost frightening intensity burned behind Leahy's blue eyes. Football was his life. After the closing game of one season, he hurried to his office and spent the entire evening studying game films. "Others are plotting," he told astonished associates. "So must we."

Winning obsessed him. A tie was a loss; a defeat a black mark against, as Leahy would say, Our Lady's name. He wanted nothing less than the best athletes, the best coaching, a perfect season, and a national championship every year.

His accomplishments displeased only the perfectionist himself. In eleven campaigns with the Irish, Leahy coached six undefeated teams, two with perfect records, and won four national titles. His statistics reveal a won-lost percentage just short of Rockne's: 87-11-9, an 88% victory bulge.

★

"He put the mist in pessimist," said the newspapers, frequently caricaturing the Notre Dame coach with crying towel in hand, tears of despair rolling down the sad Irish face. A black pessimist by nature, Leahy exaggerated his hopelessness for the press; it was his idea of colorful copy.

He usually made his pre-game statement

He could look intense while eating a cheese sandwich.

unshaven, wearing a shirt a size or two too large, appearing more haggard than he actually was after sleepless nights of preparation. "Gentlemen," he would purr softly, like a repentant felon before a magistrate, "the lads representing Our Lady's institution simply do not have the stamina to defeat the young gentlemen from [let's say] the United States Military Academy (Leahy-talk for Army). Our team is woefully unworthy to take the field against such outstanding opponents. Perhaps, ooohh, perhaps the fault is my own. I have not prepared the players as well as I should. I know I have not. Surely our boys are weak and slow, our line small and inexperienced, our runners hampered with injuries . . ." and so on.

Of course, the team Leahy had so described would storm out and butcher the unfortunates on the other side. But nothing stopped Lachrymose Leahy's gloomy predictions. Before the beginning of one season he repeatedly insisted, quite seriously, that he didn't expect his lads to get a first down all year. The team turned out to be one of his best.

★

What his players remember most are those practices. Warm up exercises and calisthenics seemed like nap-time. Frank Leahy demanded two hours of all-out, full speed, hard-hitting football every afternoon.

Loaded with the deepest talent ever seen on a college team, the high-strung coach could afford the luxury of almost daily scrimmages. Injuries? Leahy never worried about those; he had too many talented replacements sitting on the bench. Besides, he wasn't above asking a boy to play hurt. "We all need a little more Christian Scientist in us," he used to say.

Often, during the roughest scrimmages, the coach would violently shake his head. "Lads," he would whine, "what seems to be our problem? I see no blood. I see no fights. Our Lady on the dome is watching, and she must have turned her back on us in shame." Sure enough, the fights, the blood, the monster intensity that makes for winning football would come in a hurry.

Three of this era's best assistant coaches were nicknamed The Parrot, The Enforcer, and Captain Bligh. If nothing else, that should give you some idea of what it was like to play Notre Dame football in the glory years of Francis William Leahy.

★ ★ ★

One day in the early forties, the team was being drilled in the stadium. Since the new season was still months away, coaches were not permitted on the field. Instead, the entire staff sat in the press box, with Leahy barking orders at the team through a loudspeaker.

It was a typically tough practice until darkness approached and a thick fog plopped onto the playing field. With even the stands fog-bound and obscured from the players, Leahy's commands took on a surrealistic quality. The disembodied voice seemed to come from everywhere and nowhere; and it had little reference to what was actually happening on the gridiron. Leahy continued as though everything were perfectly normal. In fact, he could not see a thing.

It did not take the players long to figure this out. One by one, and in growing groups, they snided off the field and into the showers. A few fellows remained, yelping and grunting, trying desperately to sound like a whole team. At last, Leahy gave the order to run some laps and quit for the day. The left-over players jogged in small circles near the

press box, where Leahy could catch ghost-like glimpses of their fleeting figures.

Practice ended. Leahy never did seem to find out. As Winston Churchill said, "Never was so much owed by so many to so few."

★ ★ ★

Common sense was occasionally misdirected during a road trip. No one knows exactly how it happened, but about the time the rest of the team arrived in Madison, Wisconsin, for the 1942 season opener against the Badgers, Angelo Bertelli realized he was on a train headed for Keokuk, Iowa. Angelo had apparently missed signals in Chicago; a big disconcerting, inasmuch as he was supposed to be Notre Dame's starting quarterback. Somehow, Bertelli made it to Madison for the kick-off, but the Irish could only manage a 7-7 tie.

★ ★ ★

Road trips weren't all bad. One victorious JV team stopped at a roadside restaurant for dinner and had their check paid by a bashful superfan who fled out the front door before he could be thanked.

The team's coach was just a senior, an injured varsity player. He was a very responsible person in the eyes of the men, Leahy's men, who had appointed him. After discovering that the meal had already been purchased, the coach stared into his wallet at the fifty dollars he had been given to feed the team. Looking up, the coach saw every JV player smiling at him, eyes bright with anticipation. This was the coach's big chance. He could throw in his lot with the other coaches, the adults; or he could do something to make Notre Dame men everywhere stand up and cheer.

The coach pulled the fifty dollars out of his wallet. He motioned a waitress over to the table. He ordered drinks for everyone on the team. And they sat there all evening and drank through their fifty dollars and then some.

You'll get some argument, but a lot of people say this is what playing football for Notre Dame is all about.

★   ★   ★

Lou Rymkus, after a brutal Good Friday practice: "Now I think I know how Christ felt on the cross."

★   ★   ★

One of the school's most famous administrators made an impassioned speech that hit the front page of the *New York Times*. His demands were straightforward: Where are the Catholic scholars? Where are those in whom the desire for learning, for wisdom, burns brightly? Notre Dame is looking for those men!

It was an impressive address. Notre Dame's academic reputation shot up like a hot stock on Wall Street.

A few days later, the same priest was visiting friends at the Holy Cross seminary in Washington D.C. "Wait'll you get a load of this new center we got," he breathed excitedly. "Looks like an ape!" The priest stuck out his jaw and pushed a rubbery lower lip toward his nose. "Walks like an ape!" He swung his arms to his knees and loped around the room. "But, boy," the priest grinned broadly, "can he play football!"

★   ★   ★

Angelo Bertelli was the worst runner and the best passer Frank Leahy ever coached. We offer three enduring images of the Springfield Rifle, as Bertelli was aptly tagged:

Bertelli: a golden arm more than made up for feet of clay.

First, as the quarterback that helped Leahy introduce the T-formation at Notre Dame. Almost no one born after World War II has seen anything but the T or variations thereof, but when Leahy decided to use it, you would have thought he was sending the boys out there to play in roller skates. "What's wrong with the box shift?!" everyone wanted to know, usually in more colorful language than that. "It was good enough for Rockne!"

Yes, but not good enough for modern football, and it is to Leahy's everlasting credit that he broke the Irish out of a box formation that had seen much of its scoring punch legislated out of existence. The Irish went 7-2-1 in 1942, the first year of the T. By

1943, Notre Dame had a Bertelli-led T-formation national championship.

Leahy was attracted to the inherent deceptiveness of the T, the innumerable plays that could be run off the same formation. He also liked the idea of allowing his quarterback to concentrate on passing and hand-offs, and not running. This was custom-made for Bertelli, whose idea of running consisted of a slow glide that netted a little over a yard per carry.

Don't sell Bert short. He had to memorize a radically new offense and make it work against the toughest teams in the country. He was brilliant. For this alone he deserved the Heisman Trophy that was handed to him in 1943.

★

Second, there is the memory of Bertelli on ice. We're not referring to the hockey-playing Bertelli, who was so good that the Boston Bruins wanted to sign him right out of high school. We mean Bertelli dropping back in the pocket, as cool and self-assured as anyone in the stadium. A master at work, he used to look more like a big-time executive answering his mail than a 6'1" quarterback in imminent danger of getting crunched by a couple oversized tackles.

Bertelli would set up, look one way then another, flick the ball under his chin like a man shooing a fly, and suddenly let loose with another flat, accurate pass. His lifetime completion average of 52.5 is outstanding, but those who played with him always mention that he was totally unperturbable. A quarterback has no finer quality.

★

Finally, there was Bertelli the mobster. Duke, he

was called. Duke Bertelli. Armed and dangerous. There is a little touch of Irish madness that hits any student at Notre Dame when he realizes that South Bend is a long way from home. Bertelli handled the dreaded disease with a good-natured play actor's interest in gangsters. He could be seen stalking around the campus in zoot suit and floppy hat, nervously eyeing his fellow students, and always ready to go for the "gun" in his breast pocket. More often than not, he was shadowed by several similarly dressed and trigger-happy body guards.

His interest in uncommon occupations was nothing new. After accompanying his parents on a trip to their native Venice in 1921, young Bertelli protested returning to the States. He wanted to stay in Venice and become a gondolier.

★　★　★

Years later, when a serious knee injury threatened his pro career, Angelo Bertelli was wheeled into surgery, given an anesthetic, and told to count backwards from one-hundred.

"Okay," murmured Angelo. "Hundred. Ninety-nine. Ninety-eight. Hike!"

The doctor cancelled the operation.

★　★　★

"Rabbity. A trifle too rabbity," complained Coach Frank Leahy. He was talking about Creighton Miller, his magnificently talented left halfback.

Leahy's problem with Miller was simple. Miller's family was well off. Creighton Miller did not need and would not accept a football scholarship, no matter how many times Leahy tried to push one on him.

Like any coach, Leahy did not shirk from using

Creighton Miller.

scholarships to control a player. A scholarship strengthened a man's ties to his school; it gave him a sense of responsibility to his team. Also, a coach could always threaten to discontinue the scholarship. This way, the player's father would start getting bills he thought only existed in defense contracting.

Creighton Miller, happily, was unburdened by any of this. One fine April day, Frank Leahy sought out Creighton on campus.

"Will you be out for practice this afternoon?" inquired Leahy.

Creighton Miller filled his lungs with the breath of Spring. "Think I'd rather play golf today," he said.

"Ooooh, Creighton Miller!" Leahy was pained. "Football demands constant practice."

"So does golf," smiled Miller. "You'd be surprised."

Miller's presence at practice was as likely to upset Leahy as his absence. He had an annoying habit of cheering for his brother, Tom, who was also on the team. Tom cheered just as hard for Creighton.

"Atta boy, Creighty," Tom would yell during a tackling drill. "Way to bring 'em down. Great tackle!"

"Yay, Tom, what a block!" Creighton would cheer. "That's how to play football."

This was not Frank Leahy's idea of a truly disciplined football practice.

One particular drill was especially hard on the ends, who had to streak down the field, grab a punt, run back to the kicker, and repeat the whole process *ad nauseam*. The ends were lucky one day to have Creighton Miller as their punter. When they signalled that they were getting tired, Creighton was only too happy to give them a rest. He promptly kicked the ball off the side of his foot and over the fence. Everyone had to wait while a team manager retrieved the pigskin. When the ball came back, Miller hooked it over the fence again.

"Ooooh, Creighton Miller!" It was Leahy from the tower overlooking the practice field. "Surely you can kick better than that."

"Sure, Coach." Miller got another ball and winked at the ends. "Like this?" He kicked it over the fence again.

"Oh, my," gasped Leahy. "You're doing it wrong. All wrong."

Miller looped another ball out of bounds.

Leahy climbed out of the tower and rushed to Miller's side. The coach began a long technical lecture on proper punting technique.

"I got it," Miller nodded. Another ball went over the fence.

"Ooooh, Creighton Miller!" Leahy kept teaching; Miller kept squirting his kicks to the side; and the ends kept their laughter to themselves.

★   ★   ★

If you ever spent a dull day in a college dorm, well, you should have invited Creighton Miller over. Miller once bet his roommate that he could strip the wall of some three dozen pennants without using his hands. The roomie saw no harm in a little wager, and the bet was on.

Miller used his feet: kicking off the lower pennants, running up the wall and knocking out the tacks of the higher ones. Imagine his agility, scurrying up the wall like that! It must have been a marvelous sight. The only reason Miller lost the bet was that the wall collapsed on him.

Oh, he was all right. Some guys will do anything to get a larger room.

★   ★   ★

These were the war years, when the United States was engaged in the grim business of folding up the three ring circus of Hitler, Mussolini, and Hirohito. Whole corporations were going "in for the duration." Half of the Notre Dame campus had have been given over to the Navy for its V-7 training program; Frank Leahy even tore himself away from football to accept a commission with the Pacific Fleet immediately after the 1943 season. Assistant Coach Ed McKeever took over.

The most striking thing about McKeever was not the crisp grey-green eyes or the curly brown hair, but the dedication to football rivaled only by Leahy's. Like his boss, McKeever had a tendency to let football overlap into family matters, with odd results.

In 1940, McKeever was working under Leahy when Boston College headed south for the Sugar Bowl. Mrs. McKeever was about to give birth, but what did that matter? Coach McKeever had to be with his first family, the team.

No sooner did he step off the train in New Orleans than McKeever heard he was the father of twin girls. "Boys," he beamed to the team, "whoever scores a touchdown for us in the Sugar Bowl can name my girls!"

Mike Holvak and Mickey Connolly took him up on it, leading Boston College to the 19-13 win and dubbing the twins Susan Helen and Jane Ann.

Now, what if Boston College had been shut out?

★   ★   ★

Knute Rockne's pep talks worked. Frank Leahy's pep talks worked. Ed McKeever should have kept his mouth shut.

Before the 1944 Army game, McKeever told the team about his grandmother. She was sick, he confided in a soft Texas accent, and it would probably perk her up to hear the Irish play a good game that day. Her radio would be on and — weak as she was — her old, sick heart would beat for Notre Dame.

By the half, Grandma McKeever's condition had suddenly become critical. Notre Dame was being kicked all over the field and McKeever allowed as how grandma needed a close score to pull her through. Just make it respectable, he pleaded. Think of her.

Late in the game, with Army crushing Notre Dame 59-0, Quarterback Boley Dancewicz wondered aloud what play to call next. "It doesn't matter what we run any more, Boley," offered a teammate. "The old bat must be dead by now."

★   ★   ★

There are players in the right place at the right time but in the wrong position. Before the 1944 Pitt game, Tom Gutherie wowed the crowd by flinging a football 100 yards through the air. Unfortunately, Gutherie was not a quarterback. He was an end, and ends are seldom called upon to toss a football even 50 or 75 yards.

Back to the pits, Tom Gutherie.

★   ★   ★

A halfback was caught rolling ivory bones with ebony dots — shooting craps is the technical term — and hauled up before the Prefect of Discipline. The priest seethed behind his wide mahogany desk. He had already decided to toss this wicked gambler out of school. But first, the usual rhetorical question.

"What," harrumphed the Prefect, "have you ever contributed to Notre Dame?"

The halfback reached into his mouth and pulled out his false teeth — the real ones had been lost in past football wars. He dropped the store choppers on the desk without a word.

He was acquitted.

★   ★   ★

Check these Notre Dame statistics:
Dead weight tonnage .... 10,000 tons
Total displacement .... 14,900 tons
Length .... 455 feet
Speed .... in excess of 15 knots

If nothing else, the knots should tip you off that we are not describing an exceptionally well-nourished seven man line. The above stats are those of the *S. S. Notre Dame Victory,* an AP-3 type cargo ship that was launched from the Portland, Oregon shipyards in March of 1945. No other school's athletic achievements have been so honored.

★   ★   ★

Nothing like getting showered, shaved, dressing in your best suit, all-weather coat, snapped-brim fedora and Florsheim shoes — then spending the day in a shallow grave.

Besides the predictable success of the Fighting Irish and the New York Yankees, little else was constant in postwar America. Our sworn enemies, Japan and Germany, became staunch allies. Old partners, China and Russia, were deadly adversaries in something novel, a Cold War. Winston Churchill inveighed against the Iron Curtain. The Bomb hovered over all. So did Senator Joseph McCarthy, who was always threatening to produce a list of Communists, fellow travelers, sympathizers, and assorted pinkos. This lunacy spread even to Notre Dame, where a few outspoken faculty members and priests were investigated under suspicion of being "closet reds."

Harry Truman promised a Fair Deal and embarrassed the *Chicago Tribune.* Babies boomed. Bebop bleated flatted fifths. Men started smoking filter cigarettes instead of Lucky Strikes. In Europe: the Marshall Plan, the Berlin airlift, a split between East and West.

At Notre Dame: building, expansion, and black faces on campus, a change wrought by the Navy's V-7 program. In the football offices, Frank Leahy enjoyed the spoils of war. From the first game of 1946 to the second game of 1950, Notre Dame did not lose: thirty-nine games without a defeat. There were two or three National Championships mixed in there, depending upon which polls you read.

What made it all possible was World War II. For four years the armed forces had siphoned off outstanding undergraduate football players. In 1946, they all returned, with years of eligibility, to join a team that had ranked ninth nationally the year before. Frank Leahy mustered out of the Navy to face the delightful prospect of forty-two returning lettermen. In those days of one platoon football, it amounted to almost four complete, experienced teams.

★   ★   ★

Look," says the famous quarterback, "they say that Einstein couldn't make change. His mind was just too *involved* for that sort of thing. Well, Leahy was like that during a game. I mean, the guy was a genius. No one prepared as minutely as he did. You know, he was probably the first coach to use a defensive huddle. The first to develop that pass protection pocket. The first to use a screen of sideline blockers for punt returns . . . I could go on. And the way he could produce, every week, two or three super plays for that week's opponents. Hey, he was the greatest."

A grin. "But as far as most of us on the team were concerned, when some Saturdays rolled around, we much preferred Leahy had just stayed at home. There were times when he forgot where he was — what he was doing. He was just too wrapped up in everything."

A few examples:

In one Wisconsin game, Leahy called up to the press box in the middle of the second half. Jake Kline was on the other end.

"Yeah, coach," said Jake.

"Isn't it a lovely day, today?" said Leahy.

"What?" Jake glanced down to the sidelines where Leahy was talking. The coach was staring into the sky.

"The leaves changing colors, the birds taking wing over the marvelous setting of the stadium . . . and isn't the sky a beautiful color?"

Another coach in the box tapped Jake in the arm. "What's he saying?" he asked.

"Uh," said Jake, "I think he's going to go to the air."

★

In a tussle with Texas, the Irish found themselves stalled on the Longhorn thirty-five. Leahy flashed the signal for a kick, meaning a punt.

Notre Dame lined up in field goal position.

Panicked, Leahy grabbed the person next to him — a student manager who was towelling off a football — and shoved him onto the field. "Get in there and stop that play!" Leahy shouted.

The manager spurted halfway to the quarterback before he realized who and what and where he was. He wheeled and gaped at the coach. "Hey," he screamed in awe, "I can't *do* this!"

★

John Mazur was KO'ed in the 1951 Navy game and left face down in a pool of water. His teammates on the bench cried out, fearing he might drown. At last, the unconscious quarterback was hauled to the sidelines.

"Hugh Burns," shrilled Leahy, "Hugh Burns, get over here immediately with some smelling salts."

The trainer dutifully hustled over and thrust a bottle under Mazur's nose. Leahy snatched it out of his hands.

"Not for him, Hugh Burns!" Leahy took a deep snort of the pungent salts. "For me!"

★

"McManus," the coach boomed during one tight contest. "Get McManus in there."

No response.

"McManus," called Leahy impatiently, still not taking his eyes off the field.

"Coach," began a timid assistant, "there's no one named McManus on the team."

"Well, then," said Leahy, grabbing his minion by the lapels, "get somebody named McManus, get him into uniform, and get him into the game."

★   ★   ★

Leon Hart's first play in a Notre Dame uniform, in the 1946 Illinois game, was a breath-taking mixture of raw power and cat quickness. Displaying the ability that later made him a consensus All-American and Heisman Trophy winner, he drove forward with his head down and flattened the man in front of him. Unfortunately, the man in front of him was a teammate, Bob Livingstone, best described after his encounter with Leon as the unconscious Bob Livingstone.

Summoned midway through the game by Leahy, Hart had pranced eagerly forward from the bench and listened while the coach warned him against the mistakes of youth. Then, excited at being sent into the fray, the freshman end wheeled and headed full throttle for the huddle. He hardly broke stride as he steamrolled Livingstone, who was trotting off the field when the hit-and-run occurred.

Several minutes later, Livingstone came to. "Whew," he whistled, rubbing the back of his neck, "I've never been hit that hard before. That kid's going to be all right."

"Yeah," piped trainer Hughie Burns, "but first we've gotta teach him whose side he's on."

★ ★ ★

Steve Oracko has the distinction of being the only player whose injury made a coach feel good. Oracko was the Irish placekicker, an important but not irreplaceable cog in Leahy's late-forties juggernauts.

During a kick-off in the 1947 Navy game, an Irish player went down. "James Martin!" cried Leahy, averting his eyes, fearing for his star left end.

"It isn't Martin," soothed an assistant coach. "It's Oracko."

Tentatively, Leahy lifted his head.

"Coach," said someone trying to cheer him up, "it couldn't happen to a better guy."
Leahy did not disagree.
Oracko recovered.

★ ★ ★

Years later, after Flossie Leahy had suffered an accident, she phoned her husband.
"Frank," she said, "I just broke my leg."
"Oh, my," gasped the coach.
"Frank," she said, "better me than Johnny Lattner, huh?"
Leahy did not disagree.
Flossie recovered.

★ ★ ★

At a hall card party, Frank Gall remarked to Bull Budynkiewicz: "Bull, I didn't know you could whistle and deal cards at the same time."
Bull blushed. "Yeah," he admitted. "I'm ambidexterous."

★ ★ ★

There's no argument about the most versatile athlete ever to pull on pads for the Irish. His name was Johnny Lujack; he collected sports monograms like a kid saving box tops.

Look up Lujack's offensive statistics. Outstanding for sure, but they cannot do him justice. The ball-hawking Pennsylvanian's ferocious open-field tackling iced many a victory. Take the 1943 Army game, when Glenn Davis intercepted a Lujack pass and headed downfield with two blockers in front of him. Lujack alone stood between the charging Cadets and the Notre Dame goal. A bone-jarring collision: Lujack

Thaddeus J. "Bull" Budynkiewicz.

knocked down all three Cadets. A running-passing-kicking-blocking back with deadly defensive instincts, he was the closest anyone ever came to being a one-man football team.

But the best example of Lujack's athletic versatility has nothing to do with football. It all started when Coach Jake Kline's baseball team had lost five in a row.

Facing a tough tilt with Western Michigan, Kline wanted new blood in the lineup. Lujack, who had once been offered a baseball contract by the Pittsburgh Pirates, seemed the ideal tranfusion. Though already running track for the Irish, he

Play it again, Johnny. Leahy and Lujack in a Casablanca setting.

agreed to join forces with Kline's horsehide Hibernians in the next game.

Then some troublemaker pointed out that the game against Western Michigan and a dual track meet with DePauw were scheduled for the same afternoon. It looked as though Lujack would have to stick with short pants and cinders. But since the baseball game and track meet were being held at opposite ends of Cartier field, Jake Kline argued that Lujack could participate in both. Lujack sportingly agreed.

His baseball skills had not deserted him. The moonlighting quarterback turned in a faultless performance as the right field fly catcher, as well as smacking two singles and a booming triple at the plate. Each time the Irish were at bat, he trotted over to the track meet, where he took first place in the javelin toss but lost the high jump. He was disqualified after three attempts at leaping 5' 10", a height he normally cleared as easily as a man stepping over a puddle. He negotiated the jump smoothly each time, but his baggy baseball pants kept brushing the crossbar and knocking it to the ground.

By the end of the day, both Notre Dame teams were victorious. Jake Kline had snapped that dreadful five game streak with a little help from Lujack.

★　★　★

Emil Sitko missed one game because of a bad night's sleep. Somehow, during his dreams of outdistancing Lujack, Sitko wedged his foot into the frame of the bed. When he rolled over, he sprained his ankle.

★　★　★

Navy was reeling. Toward the end of the first half, the Notre Dame second string was already in the ball game and even they were driving for a score. The Middies, weary, battered, literally out of breath, needed a time-out to regroup; but they had none remaining. Glumly did the Midshipmen dig in, prepared to be overwhelmed.

All at once, Notre Dame called a time-out. Why? Irish quarterback George Ratterman was organizing a post game party. "I told this girl I'd be there," he explained to his shocked teammates. "How many of you guys can make it?"

Coach Frank Leahy swayed visibly on the sidelines. He tended to frown on things like this. They are part of the reason he started Johnny Lujack ahead of Ratterman in the Notre Dame backfield.

Like Lujack, Ratterman was a natural, a truly gifted athlete to whom even the most difficult feats were instinctive. Unlike Lujack, Ratterman was at his best when unbridled. Dissonant as a bop musician, Ratterman improvised everything: running away from his interference, passing to heavily covered receivers, telling jokes on the scrimmage line. Nimble as a magician, the angular six-footer often disdained a straight hand-off so he could slip the ball behind his back or between his legs to startled running backs. All of which impressed Frank Leahy not one bit. Leahy felt faint whenever one of his players did not respond like the X's and O's on a locker room blackboard. And with the kind of talent Notre Dame had in the post war years, the coach could afford to keep even a player of Ratterman's ability nailed to the bench.

Off the field he did not change. Whenever a car pulled into an intersection crosswalk, pedestrian Ratterman kept right on walking onto the floorboard, up the fender, across the hood, and back down. He once crawled through the backseat of a police car — unnoticed by the cops in front — rather than walk around. He could blaze new trails with a car as well as through one, like the time he tried to drive up the steps of the University administration building, giving the priests who worked in the big offices nightmares about being run over in their own waiting rooms.

One glowing moment truly captures the spirit of his football career. Years after leaving Notre Dame, Ratterman was playing professional football for the Cleveland Browns and Coach Paul Brown, a football disciplinarian who made Leahy look slack and easy going. Among other things, Coach Brown insisted on calling every play. Brown once sent a play into Ratterman. Ratterman sent it right back out.

★   ★   ★

IRISH

George Ratterman could produce a ball from thin air.

During a pressure-packed scoreless tie, Notre Dame's Bob Livingstone missed a tackle, allowing his opponent to tear off a sizable chunk of yardage.

Sky-high Johnny Lujack flew off the Irish bench. "Livingstone," he yelped, "You Son of a Bitch!"

Outraged, Leahy whirled and blasted: "Jonathan Lujack, one more profane outburst will cost you your place at Our Lady's. Cursing a comrade, indeed! You have embarrassed your parents, your school, yourself and your teammates."

Thoroughly scolded, Lujack slunk back to the bench.

On the very next play, Livingstone missed yet another tackle.

Leahy turned to the team. "Gentlemen," he bellowed, "I fear that Jonathan Lujack is right about Robert Livingstone."

★   ★   ★

Zygmont Pierre Czarobski: All-America tackle, member of the College Football Hall of Fame, fund raiser without peer. Most people, however, know him as the comic laureate of the Fighting Irish. Ziggie Czarobski: even the name is worth a laugh. A beer barrel-shaped son of a South Side Chicago butcher, he trundled down to South Bend in the Fall of 1942 with a few articles of clothing and a suitcase crammed to the seams with Polish sausage and cheese. "I don't know if they'll feed me right, and I'm not taking any chances," explained Ziggie. With that guarded judgment of the school by the lake, the reign of Zygmont the Jester was underway.

It seems that everyone who attended Notre Dame with Czarobski — in 1942 and 1943, and back again with the post war hell-raisers of 1946 and 1947 — has a favorite from that genre of anecdotes known as "Ziggie stories." Asked to speak at pep rallies, he would begin: "Reverend fathers, brothers of the bookstore, sisters of the laundry, fellow athlete scholars . . ." and proceed to keep the student body in stitches for ten minutes. Ziggie had a figure like King Farouk's and a mouth like Henny Youngman's and a penchant for hobnobbing with celebrities. When the team was on the road he would occasionally show up for breakfast with the likes of Cecil B. DeMille and actress Elizabeth Scott on his arms. "Fellas," he would greet his teammates, "I'd like you to meet my friends, Lizzy and Ceecul."

Some of the Ziggie stories are legend. When an

Ziggie tackles another audience.

exasperated Frank Leahy felt that the squad needed a return to basics, he held up a football for all to see and explained, "Gentlemen, this is a football."

"Hold it," Ziggie protested. "Not so fast, Coach."

George Connor and Ziggie once found themselves riding an elevator in New York's Waldorf-Astoria Hotel with General Omar Bradley. Bradley, recognizing the pair, mentioned how much he enjoyed Notre Dame football games. Seeking to return the great man's compliment, Ziggie cleared his throat and said, "Thanks, General. And speaking for the rest of the team . . . we sure have enjoyed your battles."

But the Leviathian of Levity's finest rejoinder may have come on a football road trip, when a friend set him up with a blind date. Ziggie was in the lobby of the team's hotel awaiting the girl. There was a tap on his shoulder. Aren't you Zygmont Pierre Czarobski?" asked a female voice.

"That's me," he said. He turned to see a girl who carried as much ballast as the *U. S. S. Ticonderoga.* Her face looked as though somebody had hit it with a shovel.

"I'm Clara, your date for tonight." Ziggie's worst fears were confirmed.

He thought quickly. "Ohhh!" he gushed. "You must be looking for the *other* Zygmont Pierre Czarobski."

★ ★ ★

Frank Leahy, replying to a suggestion that Notre Dame's success was due in part to the prayers of fans: "Prayers work better when the players are bigger."

★ ★ ★

Tree Adams was a big fellow: 6'7", 230 pounds. "Sure," said Ziggie Czarobski one day at

"Tree" Adams taking off.

practice. "Big enough to run full speed into that?" Ziggie hooked a thumb toward the high plank fence that surrounded Cartier field.

Adams wanted to think about that one.

"Betcha five bucks you're afraid to run into the fence," said Zig.

That was it. No more thinking for Adams. For five dollars he would run into anything.

The two players slinked to the sidelines and waited. When the coaches weren't looking, Adams was off.

At first, Adams lumbered toward the fence. Then he gathered speed. He charged. He darted. He flew.

SMASH! Adams bashed into the fence, his impact muffled only by the hard contact drills at the other end of the field. The fence gave way, boards spewing high into the air while Adams tumbled outside. Crazily, like a Saturday morning cartoon, enough of the boards fell back into place to close the hole. Adams, dazed, on his duff, found himself walled out of Cartier field.

Frank Leahy, intense as always, had not noticed a thing. Now he wanted his big tackle to run a few plays. "Jonathan Adams," he called. No answer. Leahy's blue eyes swept the practice field. Adams, by far the biggest man on the team, usually stuck out like a silk tie in a coal mine. Now he was gone. "My goodness," Leahy murmured to himself. "Jonathan Adams seems to have disappeared." He couldn't figure it out. The pressures of big time coaching . . . .

★ ★ ★

Leahy and his wife were late getting to the church for Johnny Lujack's wedding. George Connor, a tackle turned usher, glided over to his coach.

"You're late, Leahy," hissed Connor. "Take ten laps around the church before I seat you."

Zzzzz . . . William Fischer

Moose Fischer was one of the few Notre Dame players to have a body guard. At 6'2", 230 lbs., and as classy a left guard as the Irish ever had, Moose was not in much physical danger. He needed someone to look after him because he was liable to fall asleep anywhere at any time. Though most of us know this disease as too many early classes after too much partying, its real name is narcolepsy, and Moose had it bad. He would fall asleep at meals,

during lectures, maybe even during a date or two. On a few road trips, the team accidentally left him on the train, snoring heavily. After a series of such incidents, someone always had the job of following Moose around and keeping him awake.

Happily, Moose has now shaken the sleeping sickness entirely. Still, we would think twice before hiring him as an air-traffic controller.

★ ★ ★

When the injured Art Perry found his left leg encased in a hip to toe cast, he looked forward to a few days without football practice. No such luck.

"Leahy saw me limping across campus," recalls Perry. "He asked me how I was. I said I felt okay."

"That's good, Arthur," cooed the coach. "Because as scholarship athlete, you have certain responsibilities to fulfill. I shall expect you at practice this afternoon."

Perry went to practice. "I thought," he says, "just to watch."

Leahy had other ideas. He inquired about the leg again. "Some slight exercise might be just the tonic to improve your condition, Arthur," he offered.

Perry's parents, meanwhile, were worried and upset. Having just heard of their son's injury, they had motored to Notre Dame that very day. But Art was nowhere to be found. His room, the infirmary, the hospital — where could he be? In desperation, the Perrys hurried to football practice. They passed through the gate of Cartier field and froze. There was their injured boy, in a hip cast, running laps.

"My parents were kind of surprised," admits Perry. "They still talk about it."

★ ★ ★

Notre Dame's unbeaten streak stood at thirty-six and the Irish were driving for yet another national title when Kyle Rote started running wild in the second half of the 1949 Southern Methodist game. Rote might as well have been the whole Mustang team. He was everywhere at once: running, passing, blasting the line, swiftly sticking enough points on the board to knot the game at 20-20 with only minutes remaining.

Notre Dame took the kick-off and drove furiously downfield. The Cotton Bowl's all-time loudest crowd was splitting the Texas sky with cheering and hooting and clanging cowbells. Quarterback Bob Williams called a quick time-out. The entire Irish offensive unit scurreid to the bench.

"Well, Coach," demanded Williams, "do you have any advice?"

"Yes, Robert," intoned Leahy solemnly. He thought a moment, then: "Never enter the coaching profession."

The entire Irish offensive unit scurried to the bench.

★ ★ ★

Midway through this frenzied contest, a giant tackle wheeled into a crushing cross-body block. After the whistle, his Southern Methodist opponent picked himself up and huffed, "Nice block, y'all."

The Irish tackle burned. "Y'all, hell," he said. That was *me.*"

★ ★ ★

It was the Iowa game of 1951. Placekicker Bobby Josephs got a leg cramp. Not serious in itself, but Coach Leahy was adamant: injuries had to be held to a minimum. To avoid complications, Donny

Bianco, a reserve guard, was instructed to massage the cramp. Bianco threw himself on Josephs' leg. Bianco massaged it with great vigor. He massaged it so hard he dislocated his own shoulder.

★　★　★

An Irish touchdown in the 1952 Pitt game made the score 20-19. The point after touchdown, a foregone conclusion, would tie the score.

Notre Dame made ready for the extra point. Center Jim Schrader cradled the football in his hands. At the signal, he would hike the ball back seven yards. Minnie Mavraides, the kicker, stared at the goalposts. In his mind, he repeated the rhythm of the kick over and over. Tom Carey would receive the snap from center and hold for the kick. Tom was loose. A few seconds before the hike, he turned his head and looked up to say something to Mavraides.

Instead, Tom's mouth dropped open and stayed open. This is because he saw the football flying high over his head. Jim Schrader had made a very bad hike at a very wrong time.

You have to love games like this, because they are what made Frank Leahy's reputation. By the time Schrader had slinked back to the bench, Leahy was twitching with anger and frustration.

Understandably, Schrader was sobbing. Leahy loomed over him. "Ooooooo, you, James Schrader," shrieked the coach. "You didn't want the noble school of Notre Dame to win today. You're from Pittsburgh. You have friends in the stands. That is why you have embarrassed Our Lady."

Schrader was almost hysterical by now. But Leahy was hardly finished. The coach often mixed religion and football. Sometimes they came out wrong.

Leahy's neck was quivering, his face crimson. As he talked, he poked Schrader in the nose with a sharp, bony finger to emphasize every word. "James Schrader," barked Leahy, *"you'll burn in hell for this!"*

Through his tears, Schrader could only manage: "I know, Coach. I *know!*"

Light a candle for Jim Schrader tonight.

★　★　★

Leahy, when asked the sex of his newly-born baby: "Fullback."

★　★　★

"You can do more recruiting by drying dishes in the kitchen with a boy's mother than you can with all the promises in the world." Leahy proved his own quaint theory by getting Ralph Guglielmi enrolled at Notre Dame after a brief chat with Ralph's grandmother.

After the coach drove away from the Guglielmi home in Grandview, Ohio, Ralph's grandmother spoke in Italian — she could speak nothing else.

"That's a nice man," she told her grandson, a highly touted high school quarterback. "You should go to college where he teaches."

"Grandmother," Ralph was confused. "How can you say that? I saw you talking to Coach Leahy, but he can't speak Italian and you speak no English. How can you tell he's a nice man?"

Grandmother Guglielmi tapped her temple. "He speaks with his *eyes*," she said.

★　★　★

Johnny Lattner was not so easily secured. Leahy figured he had the prep school star safely wrapped

in green, but he had to make sure. The coach called his friend, Hughie Mulligan, a union official in Chicago: "Hugh, I'm a trifle concerned about young John Lattner. Unscrupulous coaches might attempt to dissuade him from attending our fine institution. Might you get the lad a summer job where he would be free from such annoyances?"

Mulligan promised to see what he could do.

That summer, Lattner worked at Argonne Laboratories, a top secret nuclear testing facility west of the city. He worked in a high security area. And — you guessed it — only one football coach in the country could get clearance to see him.

★　★　★

The aftermath of a 35-0 defeat at Michigan State found Leahy supine on the team's equipment trunks, a white towel draped across his face.

"Frank." It was Father Sheedy, the team captain. "Frank, do you feel ill?"

The coach pinched the lower corners of the towel and lifted it slowly until his eyes met Sheedy's. "Father," he croaked, "didn't you see the game?" And he lowered the towel back into place.

★

It was the worst loss Leahy had ever suffered; and he let the team know about it the next Monday.

"I'm calling in the F.B.I.," he announced. "I'm well aware that you players threw that game to the gamblers. And I have forbidden Frank Junior to return to campus. I won't have him associating with low-life mobsters of your ilk."

★

Obviously, straight facts and understated emotions were rare commodities when Leahy addressed his players.

"Those pre-game pep talks were the best," grins an old team captain. "I'll never forget my first game at Notre Dame. The coach walked in. Looked terrible. Looked like he had been locked in a closet all week. I had to strain to hear him. He said he had just been to the hospital. Frank Junior was dying.

"Well, of course, everyone stomped out and gave his all for Frank Junior. But we never heard another thing about him.

"Next week, Leahy trickles in and tells us his brother is at death's door. The next week, it was another of the kids. Jeez, by the end of the season, he'd killed off his whole family!"

★ ★ ★

You need a little something extra to play football at Notre Dame. For some it is courage; for others, zeal. And for a select few, it just takes being goofy.

The gang of Lee Getschow, Neil Worden, Big Joe Katchik, and Bobby Josephs fits that last category. They did some, uh, pretty unusual things together.

In the Notre Dame administration building, there is a rotunda. Three stories up is a walkway with a railing. This was too much for our boys to pass up. They took turns doing handstands on that railing, trying to see who could stay up the longest. Down below, students and instructors twisted their unrisked necks for a look at the daredevils, who went blithely about taking their lives into their own handstands. It got to be a regular event between classes, sort of a three-story circus. It's a wonder Ed Sullivan never picked up the act for his *Toast of the Town* television show.

Then there was the time Lee, Big Joe, Bobby, and Neil decided to jump off one of South Bend's busy bridges into the St. Joseph River.

We asked one of the quartet about this.

"That's nothing," he scoffed. "We jumped from all sorts of places. Cliffs and such. We'd try practically anything."

So the bridge was a small challenge?

"Well," the man smiled, "that's what we thought at first."

The four stood on the Michigan Avenue bridge and peered into the swirling waters below. Bobby, showing a modicum of common sense, backed off. But Neil, Lee and Big Joe went over the side and into the drink.

Neil and Lee popped up immediately and swam to shore. They looked back for Big Joe and saw him far out in the river. The big man surfaced in a gasp of air, then sunk out of sight. Bobby, watching from the bridge, ran for help. Big Joe bobbed up twice more. Neil and Lee sniffed trouble and waded back into the stiff current.

They searched frantically for the spot where their friend had last gone under. Big Joe suddenly splashed up in front of them. "Help me!" he spluttered. "I lost my shoe down there and I can't find it."

Now, coaches have a rather decided distaste for losing players to injuries suffered while hand-standing and bridge-jumping. Neil Worden was especially irreplacable at the time. Lee, Bobby, and Big Joe were finally warned to stay away from the hard-driving fullback — for the good of the team. But the four were inseparable. The warning had no effect.

Cuckoos of a feather . . . .

★ ★ ★

The following is a conversation that could take place today in any number of business establishments on Chicago's West Side:

"Chris, do ye remember a lad named Johnny Lattner?"

"Are ye daft, Patrick? O' course I remember Lattner. Played at Fenwick High, na five minutes from where we're sittin' now."

"Oh, he was a good one, tha' lad. They say he was the best e'er to come out o' Chicago."

"Went to Notre Dame, did he not?"

"He did. An' e'ery Irishman in the neighborhood was glad to hear it. The celebratin' went on for days."

"Ye fell off a barstool and broke yer hand."

"My right one. Tha's why I drink with my left to this very day."

"Tell me, Pat, did ye e'er see Lattner play at Notre Dame?"

"Many a time, Chris, many a time. The lad was a thoroughbred. He was faster than blazes and stronger than a damn bear. But listen here, I'll tell ya wha' made him great. It was his concentration. When he was playin' football, nothin' else entered his head."

"Like you when ye're drinkin' whiskey, eh Patrick?"

"Enough o' that, or ye'll get an extra hole in yer nose. Now order us a couple beers, and I'll tell ye a couple stories about Lattner. There were a few times when his mind wasn't in the game — against Purdue in 1952 he fumbled the ball five times."

"Five times! That Irishman they had for a coach must've thrown a fit."

"He did. Leahy made Lattner carry a football for a week, wherever he went — in th' shower, anyplace. And ye better believe Lattner did it."

"Must've been a sight. Jay-naked in the shower with a football in his hand. Bet he ne'er fumbled like that again."

"He didn't. Tha' game was an exception, because normally his concentration was wicked. But let me tell ye about a time when he was concentratin' so hard it embarrassed him."

"Wha' do ye mean, Pat?"

"I believe it was in th' Pittsburgh game of 1952. Lattner ran the ball and got his jersey ripped clean from his back, so he came back to the bench for a new one. I was watchin' him. His eyes ne'er left the field. He was concentratin' — ye know? They gave him the shirt, and when he went to put it on, he forgot all abou' where he was . . . and dropped his pants clear to his ankles!"

"No!"

"My right hand to God."

"Jay-naked again, with 50,000 fans lookin' on."

"Ohh, e'eerybody i' the crowd had a good laugh. Then a manager saw him, an' tried to co'er him up with a towel no bigger than a handkerchief. Good God, I thought I'd break a rib!"

"Oh, what a story, Pat! I haven't laughed so hard since they had to call the Fire Department t' get Tommy Fitzpatrick out of the tree."

"It is a fine story, isn't it?"

"An' it proves one thing."

"What?"

"Notre Dame players really do get more exposure than anyone in college football."

"I'll drink to that."

★ ★ ★

Time and again, Frank Leahy watched Johnny Lattner, hampered by a sore ankle, plow futilely into the 1953 Oklahoma line. He turned to coach Bill Early, at whose insistence Lattner was in the line-up. "Oooohh, Coach Early," he said, wagging a sarcastic finger at the field, "there's your All-American."

Moments later the Irish went on defense. Sooner quarterback Buddy Leake suckered the entire Notre Dame line and flipped a screen pass to Carl Allison, who had a convoy of blockers in front of him. Only the bum-ankled Lattner was in the way. But Lattner shot through the blockers like a shark through a school of halibut and bumped Allison to the turf. No gain.

Leahy felt a tug at his sleeve. "Coach Leahy," said Bill Early, "*there* is my All-American."

★ ★ ★

"Notre Dame points for nobody," said Frank Leahy, "because everybody points for Notre Dame."

★ ★ ★

Heisman Trophy winner Johnny Lattner (l.) learning the ropes.

On the morning of an important game, the coach escorted his team to the cemetery where Knute Rockne was buried. All knelt at the grave of the fallen coach. Suddenly, out of the corner of his eye, Leahy spotted two players praying at the grave of George Koegan, Notre Dame's former basketball coach.

"Lads," cried Leahy. "Lads, for heaven's sake! We can always pray for Coach Koegan during basketball season."

★　★　★

Frank Varrichione grabbed the back of his leg and squealed. He flopped to the ground in a dead faint. He looked like a man hit by a strychnine blowdart.

The day was freezing cold and blindingly sunny; the game was Notre Dame vs. Iowa. Two seconds left in the first half, Hawkeyes on top 7-0, and the Irish stalled twelve yards away from paydirt. An utterly improbable upset was in the making.

That's when Varrichione went down. It was a well-done act, and a week later he would get a replica of the Oscar from the USC football team for his starring role in the old faked-injury-to-buy-time routine. Everybody in the stadium knew Varrichione's sudden illness was a fraud. It was common practice in those days, as common as a quarterback today floating the ball out of bounds to stop the clock. No referee, however, is likely to kick a man in the ribs and growl: "Stand up. You ain't hurt." The clock froze while Varrichione was helped off the field.

This was all the time Ralph Guglielmi needed to line up his players and shoot a pass to Dan Shannon in the Iowa end zone. 7-7 at the half. On the sidelines, Iowa Coach Forest Evashevski looked as though he had just been bitten by the family terrier.

The tie stuck until Iowa scored with two minutes left in the fourth quarter. That made it 14-7, and Forest Evashevski almost permitted himself a smile. The year's biggest upset was back in the bag.

Neil Worden lugged the Hawkeye kick-off twenty-one yards to the Notre Dame forty-two yard line. Two passes later, the Irish were on the Iowa forty-six, with 1:15 on the timer.

Then, quickly:

Guglielmi passed to Lattner at the twenty-eight.

Guglielmi to Heap at the twenty.

Guglielmi to Lattner at the nine.

Forest Evashevski found his eyes drawn irresistibly to the clock. Thirty-three seconds remaining. He peered into the ice-blue sky. No, he knew, lightning couldn't strike twice.

Don Hunter and Art Penza fainted, a la Varrichione. Both were escorted off the field.

Two missed passes left a short breath on the clock.

Guglielmi bawled out the signals, nine yards away.

Forest Evashevski fidgeted. Nightmares like this don't repeat, he told himself.

Guglielmi felt the snap smack into his hands. He dropped back, faked left, and fired right to Shannon in the end zone. The conversion was good. 14-14 with six seconds remaining. And then the game was over.

On the Iowa bench, Forest Evashevski had the look of a man who had just discovered the family terrier had rabies.

★

This game doomed the faked injury routine forever. A firestorm of ciriticism sizzled across the nation's sportspages. Evashevski complained bitterly about being "cheated at Notre Dame," though he regularly instructed his boys to drop like swatted flies when time was running out. As we mentioned, every coach did.

What burned in this game was that the fraud had worked twice to perfection. And the Irish, who generally beat everybody just by playing fair, were suddenly winning with trickery. New rules were handed down: feigned faints and clock-stopping injuries strictly forbidden. It was reminiscent of the hassle over the Rockne shift. When the other schools found themselves unable to cope with it, or use it, they outlawed it.

★　★　★

The 1953 season ended with an old-style 40-14 route of SMU; but Frank Leahy appeared terribly aged and tired and sick. The fiery intensity that had made him such a successful coach had worn his health to a dangerously low level. The doctors confirmed what his family and friends were already suggesting: he might not survive another season.

Most unwillingly, the coach resigned. The Leahy era, the awesome era, was ended. The dream of a lifetime was finished.

★　★　★

Twenty years later, Leahy was dead. The coach's most famous players were his pallbearers. It was a long, steep walk from hearse to gravesite, and Johnny Lattner slipped while carrying the coffin. "Just like the coach," someone whispered. "Still riding our ass."

★　★　★

VIII.
From Scoreboard to Billboard

The *Spirit of Notre Dame* ("Dedicated to Football's Immortal Knute Rockne," according to Universal Studios) reeled out of Hollywood in October of 1931, about the time the great coach's memory was seeding a myth. And actually, J. Farrell MacDonald does a creditable job as Rockne, though the meat of his role consists of grimacing on the sidelines and delivering locker room lines like, "When the team's in a tough spot today, pull one out of the bag for Old Truck."

Old Truck is our hero. He goes to the prom and fans himself with the tails of his evening jacket. That's the highlight of the movie for us. The rest of the flick involves a character named the Hockerville Flash, who learns to enjoy being a blocking back while leading the team to a last second victory over Army. This saves Old Truck's life . . . but why go into that here?

The only engaging aspect of this show, in 1931 and today, is the presence of so many old Rambler stars, from the Four Horsemen to Bucky O'Connor. Frank Carideo is especially captivating. He appears to be always restraining himself, with difficulty, from breaking out in whoops of laughter.

Barring an incredibly misguided film festival, the only way you could see *The Spirit of Notre Dame* today is on the late show. The movie is barely bearable in an uninterrupted screening. The thought of it cut up every five minutes by commercials for rock record collections and vegetable slicer-dicers is enough to make Frank Carideo break down and cry.

★ ★ ★

When Frank Leahy introduced his brother to Pat O'Brien, Jack Leahy flashed a wide smile and extended a hand. "I could never forget the great actor who played Father Flannigan in *Boy's Town*,'

he declared.

"Oh," said Pat O'Brien, "that was Spencer Tracy."

"Well," Jack Leahy replied, "I'm positive that had they given you the part, you would have done fine."

Except for Frank Leahy's brother, when just about anyone else thinks of Knute Rockne, they likely as not produce a mental image of Pat O'Brien. He was that good in *Knute Rockne — All American*.

It's a better than average Hollywood biography, that is, a true story told fictionally. So much of Rock's life reads like romance anyway, the dream-makers had an easy time of it. Still, myths and legends, delightful lies about Notre Dame abound because of this thoroughly diverting flick. The school is portrayed as a sort of Schwabb's Drugstore of the gridiron, where every student tries out for the team, hoping to be discovered kicking a football into oblivion and suddenly transformed into an All-American.

Ronald Reagan is riveting as Gipp. He has that freshly scrubbed gee-whiz wholesomeness act down pat. It's great for impressing one-eyed voters, but it's no more like Gipp than the Hockerville Flash.

★ ★ ★

Recently, the image has not fared as well. Take *John Goldfarb, Please Come Home*. Nothing is so painful to sit through as a self-described mad-cap romp that instead limps along with the pace of a Woody Hayes offense. William Peter Blatty was guilty of the script, which loosely involved the Notre Dame team with a U-2 pilot and some harem girls. Not content with irritating the C.S.C.'s, Blatty later penned *The Exorcist* to get in some digs at the Jesuits. What he will do next to the Dominicans is anybody's guess.

A winner: Pat O'Brien as the Rock.

Did we say irritating? Notre Dame disliked the movie so much they sought an injunction against its release, thus providing this sure-fire flop with reams of free publicity. What "Banned in Boston" did for *Lady Chatterly's Lover,* Father Hesburgh's lawyers did for Goldfarb. Except that you can spend a minute or two with *Lady Chatterly* without getting the urge to switch to something like TV reruns of *Wally's Workshop.*

★   ★   ★

At this writing, two new Notre Dame movies are in the planning stage, but that's standard procedure. Quite a few have been researched and dropped. References to school and team will always pop up, some good, some bad. The movie *Looking for Mister Goodbar* tried to sketch the twisted religious fervor of a neurotic Catholic by having the character wear a Notre Dame jacket around the house. Ah, yes, film as insight; and failing that, a cinematic cheap shot.

★   ★   ★

Knute Rockne and All That Jazz is the only legitimate theater vehicle about Notre Dame. It's a Broadway musical that never made it out of South Bend, with good reason.

The cast of characters includes the Four Horsemen, Chicago gangsters, a beautiful young ingenue, and a cleft-chinned gridder named Frankie O'Rourke. The plot stumbles along like a summer camp skit; the song lyrics sound best when hummed.

The play was never produced, Broadway angels undoubtedly sensing that it would run about as long as Earl Campbell did against the Notre Dame defense. *Knute Rockne and All That Jazz* may be the reason John Goldfarb left home in the first place.

★   ★   ★

IX.
Alumni Bored
1954-1963

Notre Dame football mirrored the fifties: boring mediocrity. What else can be said of the age of hula hoops and Davy Crockett caps? Saddle shoes and ankle bracelets? Sputniks and beatniks?

Rock and roll one-four-fived its way into the AM radio consciousness of American youth. Every family bought a television: small, grey, flickering images of Uncle Miltie and Jack Lescoulie, Arthur Godfrey and Arthur Murray.

Movies were in trouble, as witness the rash of *I Was a Teenage* (Fill in the Blank With the Monster of Your Choice) movies; and grown adults wearing cardboard "3-D" glasses to get the impression of being run over by a locomotive that popped out of a movie screen. Thank goodness for the packaged goodness of Doris Day.

In sports, Brooklyn lost the Dodgers; everyone lost to the Yankees; an overtime victory for the Baltimore Colts made pro football a hot item.

The "I Like Ike's" beat out the "I'm Madly for Adlai's" and put a golfer in the White House. Vice-President Richard M. Nixon was a Notre Dame Senior Class Fellow. Martin Luther King began a long, long march.

The United States swung from Korean War to uneasy peace, from wide lapels to skinny ties, from highway to freeway, from city to suburb. But except for the pelvis of Elvis and the rejuvenated Count Basie band, very little in the fifties really swung at all. Certainly not Notre Dame. Between 1954 and 1963, they sauntered to an eleven-year log of fifty-one wins and forty-eight losses.

Ho-hum.

★ ★ ★

De-emphasis is a dirty word in the high-ceilinged administration offices under the gold dome. We never intended to cut back our football program,

say the Holy Cross priests who run the school. But when you replace the most successful coach in the country with a twenty-five-year-old high school teacher, Terry Brennan by name, it sets people to wondering.

There have been some great names in Notre Dame football: for instance Hercules Bereolos, Armando Galardo, and Jerry Ransavage. (Imagine the headlines: "Ransavage Ran Savage!")

But the above ineffectual looking halfback owned the ultimate moniker: Rockne Morrissey. He never lived up to the billing.

An old pupil of Frank Leahy's and University President Hesburgh's, Terry Brennan was smart, handsome and personable. He was also too young, inexperienced, and woefully misplaced. He was fired after a five-year record of 32-18-0.

★ ★ ★

To the new coach's dismay, Frank Leahy kept close ties with Notre Dame football after his retirement in 1953. Brennan was anxious to chop his own notch in the coaching profession; Frank, it seemed, was always dulling the ax blade. Leahy's unsolicited opinions cropped up often in the press. And while Brennan watched uneasily, his predecessor showed up at the 1954 Texas game and delivered a brief halftime sermon to the team. Players' old loyalties lingered, spiking the squad with pockets of dissension which undercut Brennan's authority. Terry was the new chief, but the Old Master hovered wistfully about, tasting the soup, suggesting recipes. "Believe me, it's no picnic having him around," Brennan once admitted.

The testy relationship between the coaches came to a head during the 1956 season. In the midst of what was to be a 2-8 year, the rumor got started that Leahy would return to Notre Dame in an "advisory capcity" for the 1957 spring practice. When contacted, Leahy said that no such offer had been extended, but that he "wouldn't mind" returning to his alma mater in such a role.

"Not as long as I'm coach, he's not," Brennan maintained.

Then, the week before the Irish wrapped up their season at Southern Cal, Leahy and Brennan fought a verbal tug-of-war over Paul Hornung. Leahy wanted Hornung as a guest on his syndicated TV show. The appearance would have violated team policy, so Brennan nixed the idea. Miffed, Leahy lashed back with a public statement:

"The old Notre Dame attitude is gone," he told reporters. "They're going down, but not going down swinging like they did in the past." He spoke at length about the lack of fight in the Irish, and speculated why it was missing.

Leahy later apologized, and the pair made up, but the damage had been done. Sensing bad blood, the national press had swooped down for the kill, and news of the quarrel clattered out on teletypes from Woodstock to Walla-Walla. 'Twas an embarrassing week for the Irish.

It was left for Sports Information Director Charlie Callahan to sum up the whole awkward affair. "None of these things," he mused, "happen when you're winning."

★   ★   ★

Players below Brennan's third team referred to themselves as "The Restayez." That, they say, is what the coaches always called them.

★   ★   ★

Even as student memories of Paul Hornung's gridiron exploits fade away, remembrances of his night-life escapades linger faintly on the Notre Dame campus. "This," a freshman will be told by an Upperclassman Who Knows, "is the fire escape where Paul Hornung used to sneak in after curfew." Tales of the Golden Boy's ability to perform on Saturday after partying like a Viking on Friday still abound.

Nobody ever had it over the young Louisvillian in the social department. "The seniors were each assigned a freshman to look after for the first few weeks in the fall," remembers a teammate.

"Hornung was my freshman. One night I was going to give him a treat, take him out to some of South Bend's night spots. Before that evening was through, he was leading *me* around to places that I didn't even know *existed.*"

★   ★   ★

When Notre Dame lined up for a field goal attempt at the twenty-nine yard line, there was a loud groan from the Irish contingent in Philadelphia's Municipal Stadium. Some of the fans decided to trot out and start their cars for the long drive home. Some legged it for a bus or train. Others sat in numb disbelief. Monty Stickles was going to try a field goal.

On the other side of the field, Army rooters hooted in unison. (The Army does everything in unison, even hoot.) Cadets nervously fingered their caps. Nothing thrills a Cadet so much as tossing his hat in the air after a well-fought football victory. Birds all over Philadelphia were chirping warnings to each other to fly clear of Municipal Stadium. The air would soon be ablaze with the ack-ack fire of Cadet caps. Monty Stickles was going to try a field goal.

Down on the gridiron, Stickles squinted at the crossbar. It was forty yards away. Under normal circumstances, a kicker would run through a little mental routine, preparing to boot the ball as he had so many times in practice. Stickles knew no such routine. He had never kicked a field goal before in his life.

Stickles was an end — one of the best. He had never claimed to be a kicker, but he helped out when he could. For all his good intentions, he had flashed as much talent with the toe as Jack Benny did with the violin. Stickles had attempted four points after touchdown, missed three. One of those

PATs had come only minutes earlier, and provided the margin of Army's 21-20 lead.

And now, the hike.

Stickles swung his foot. The ball took flight.

It was the kick of a man who had never attempted a field goal in game or practice, never even fooled with the idea back at high school in Poughkeepsie, New York.

Ninety-five thousand watched. This boot would decide the first Army-Notre Dame game in ten years.

Stickles had to angle the ball.
It angled.
It needed plenty of height.
It soared.
It had to have distance.
It got it.
The kick was good.

The Irish side erupted; the Army rooters sounded like a deflated inner tube. Disappointed Cadets screwed their hats on a bit tighter, and pigeons returned to Municipal Stadium in absolute safety.

And the guy who left to get home early? We hope he got a flat tire.

★   ★   ★

After Pittsburgh's stunning victory in 1958 — the Panthers had iced the game at 29-26 by scoring a touchdown with eleven seconds remaining — Moose Krause was ankling across the field toward the Irish dressing room when he was stopped by an alumnus.

"How many students do we have at Notre Dame?" asked the alum.

Happy to meet a fan who was not complaining about the game's bitter conclusion, Moose amiably replied, "About fifty-five hundred."

"Well," said the alum, "would it be asking too

much to put a couple of them in front of the ball carrier?"

★   ★   ★

A few years after leaving Notre Dame, Ralph Guglielmi was pitching pigskins for the Washington Redskins. The artful Gugli was not at his best for the Skins. His offensive line crumbled as easily as pound cake, and the ex-Irish star was often sacked before getting a pass away.

One practice found Gugli lying flat on his back flipping spirals into the air. Redskin Head Coach Joe Kuharich hurried over. "Whaddya think you're doing down there?" he snarled.

Explained Guglielmi: "I spend so much time on the ground, I figure I ought to start learning to pass from here."

★   ★   ★

When Terry Brennan trudged away through the snows of Christmas, 1958, the old guard returned. He was Joe Kuharich, a South Bend native and hard-nosed right guard from the Layden years, rated one of the NFL's top coaches.

Joe didn't find the finest material in the world waiting for him. In the early fall of 1959, he confided to about four thousand well-wishers at a Chicago Touchdown Club luncheon: "We have halfbacks so small they could run under this table. Without ducking." A few years at Notre Dame, and Joe would be the one wanting to duck under a table.

★   ★   ★

The 1959 Irish were the greenest in anyone's memory, at least in terms of experience. Joe Kuharich was starting with only thirteen returning lettermen. A 5-5 season, everyone said, would be tolerable. Joe was tolerable. Half-way through the 1959 campaign, there was a saying you heard just about everywhere: "The magic number for Notre Dame is 1960."

In 1960, the Irish were 2-8.

★   ★   ★

On the road to obscurity, somewhere beyond Joe Kuharich's last string team, beyond the water boys, beyond the groundseepers, were the no-names. These were the players on whom Kuharich had simply given up. After calisthenics, they were no longer asked to participate in practice. They were shunted to the far end of Cartier Field and icily ignored.

More often than not, the no-names passed the time with touch football games. The dead-end exiles actually organized a league one year, with a weekly four game round robin. Occasionally, the touch football became so boisterous, the no-names whooping it up over a touchdown pass or blocked kick, that practice screeched to a halt. Regular players froze in their scrimmaging and gaped over at their boyishly playful comrades. Then a whistle would blow: Kuharich's players would get back to work; the no-names would get back to play.

★   ★   ★

Inexperienced, highly nervous, Norb Rascher trotted out before the national TV cameras to replace George Haffner against Northwestern. The intricate duties of a signal-caller muddled in his brain. A quarterback must be cool-headed. A quarterback must be decisive. A quarterback must be deceptive. Norb Rascher was about to give a lesson in how to be none of the above.

In the huddle he babbled out what he thought was a call for a pass over the middle. Mostly it was gibberish. But ten calmer heads understood what play the newcomer had in mind.

At the line of scrimmage it dawned on Norb that he hadn't made complete sense in the huddle. He was struck with sudden, awful visions of ten teammates running ten different plays. And on national TV, yet. Panic set in. "Hey, Brian," he hissed at Brian Boulac, his intended receiver, "you know the play?"

Brian Boulac before the crunch.

The Northwestern defense had seen uncertainty in this young buck's eyes. And now they knew. Rascher's query to his receiver was a blatant tip-off, like a neon arrow indicating who was going to get the ball. Five Wildcats promptly lined up over Boulac; the other six dug in for a pass rush.

At the snap of the ball Boulac got buried. And Norb Rascher? Well, they say that parts of his body are still out there on Northwestern's field.

★   ★   ★

The sportswriter was strolling down Notre Dame Avenue on his way to Friday afternoon football practice when he stopped dead in his tracks, did a double-take, then squinted to make sure he was seeing right. He was. There, preparing to tee off on Notre Dame's golf course, was Daryle Lamonica.

Daryle Lamonica eyeballing the camera.

Lamonica was usually the first one out to practice; and it was no secret that he was unhappy with the Notre Dame program. Maybe, thought the writer, the sonofagun has quit the team. He stepped over to the fence adjoining the tee. "Hey, Daryle, aren't you going to practice?" he asked.

"Why should I?" asked the California-bred quarterback. "We only have two plays, and I know both of them."

"That mean you're not going?"

"Nah. I'll be there." Lamonica grinned. "I've got to find out which one we're using tomorrow in the game."

★   ★   ★

As Doug Seis pulled himself onto the windowsill, a vision of football practice flashed before him. It was obvious, Seis knew, that he would never make even the third team. He was standing on the ledge outside now; the wind was kissing his face, tempting him, luring him into mid-air. Seis decided to think no more of football.

He jumped.

He screamed. He fell three stories.

He landed on his feet and rolled expertly across the ground.

Doug Seis popped up and brushed the dry leaves and twigs off his shoulders. He trotted back to Zahm Hall for another leap. Football was totally out of his mind now; football was boring. Doug Seis was practicing for a position that he really desired: paratrooper for the United States Special Forces.

★   ★   ★

More than one newspaper typesetter retired early in the fall of 1960 rather than face this

potential Notre Dame backfield: Ed Rutkowski, quarterback; Ray Ratkowski, halfback; Joe Perkowski, fullback. Kuharich's stubborn refusal to play this typographical trio probably bought him a year's good press.

He needed it.

★   ★   ★

Practice was hot. Tempers were short. Hugh Devore called to his freshman footballers: "Run that play one more time."

The eager young Irish lined up. The ball was snapped. The play was botched.

"Aughhh!" cried Devore, or words to that effect. Scarlet invective blasted from his cheeks, nothing more nor less than the kind of language you hear on golf courses throughout America.

"Coach!" hissed a student manager urgently.

Devore floated immediately over to the nuns. He was charming. He apologized, profusely, for the been stuffed with cotton.

Devore floated immediately over to the nuns. he was charming. He apologized, profusely, for the nasty slip of the lip. Was there a play the sisters would like to see? Any play? The boys would run one for them.

The sisters suggested a pass.

"Action pass," shouted Devore to his students.

The play was botched.

Forgetting himself, Devore let loose with another stream of oaths. He whirled in time to see the nuns shuffling out, single file.

One football player turned to another. "Are they leaving because of the way coach talks," he asked, "or the way we play?"

★   ★   ★

Before another long season began, Joe Kuharich was asked his team's chances for the fall. Said Joe: "I know the coaches are ready. But are the boys?"

Joe Kuharich scowls at a goal line stand.

★ ★ ★

In the heat of a game, Kuharich was hit by a bit of offensive inspiration. "Carollo, come here," he growled at his huge tackle, Joe Carollo. "Take this play to the huddle . . . ." The coach proceeded to rattle off a play so full of "slants," "waggles," "staggers," and other football jargon that it made Carollo's eyes water.

"Say it again, coach," said Carollo.

Kuharich said it again. And again. Each time it slipped away from Carollo like a long and elusive strand of spaghetti. The coach finally grabbed a pad of paper, wrote down the play, and jammed it under his tackle's nose. "Here," he fumed. "Read it to them."

Carollo lumbered out to the huddle and did as he was told. His teammates called a time-out. They spent the entire minute laughing.

★ ★ ★

Ray Ratkowski was hit in the face during a scrimmage and fell to the ground, his hands covering his eyes. "Gene, Gene," he bawled. "I can't see!"

Trainer Gene Paszkiet walked onto the field. He gently pulled Ratkowski's hands away from his face.

"How's that?" said Paszkiet.

"Oh," Ratkowski blinked up at him. "Much better."

★ ★ ★

An Irish coach was a fanatic disciple of self-conditioning. One day, he gathered his players around him. "Watch this," he ordered.

WHAM! He threw himself to the ground, landing flat on his stomach. He quickly wheeled to his feet. "It's all in the muscles," he proudly announced,

tapping his rock-hard belly.

"Now, again."

WHAM! He smashed himself to the earth.

"I don't want any man on my team who can't do this," he said, pulling himself up. "It's an important exercise. I could do it all day.

"Again."

WHAM!

"Again."

WHAM! This time the coach smacked the ground with such force that he knocked himself out.

So much for that day's practice.

★ ★ ★

The kind of apathy Joe Kuharich's coaching spread across campus is best exemplified by the send-off the team received before the 1961 Iowa trip. As usual, the Notre Dame *Scholastic* urged everyone to turn out and bid a rousing farewell to the players who would be loading into big buses on Notre Dame Avenue. Rockne's teams used to get the hale and hearty from every student, every teacher on campus.

On November 24, 1961, one man showed up to wave goodbye to the Fighting Irish. He was Father Glenn Boarman. He had to be there. He was the team chaplain.

After Kuharich's kiddie corps got whompstomped 42-21, one man was waiting to welcome the team home: Father Boarman.

★ ★ ★

1961 was an upside-down year. That is, if you turn the date "1961" upside-down, it still reads "1961." The Irish celebrated this calendrical quirk with a sideways season of 5-5. The record reads correctly from either direction.

Was it some innate sense of fairness, some unconscious desire to spread victory equally between the Irish and their opponents? Kuharich apparently enjoyed going 5-5. He did it again in 1962. Then he quit. The alumni's insatiable appetite for victory bothered him, he said. It was life in a pressure cooker and it wasn't worth it.

Joe's four-year stats of 17-23 make him Notre Dame's one and only losing coach. Which is a hell of a way to be remembered. So we won't dwell on it. We'll just move on . . . .

★ ★ ★

Arunas Vasys had made up his mind. From 200 offers for football scholarships he was going to choose Illinois'. There was no need, he told his parents, for further discussion. The Ohio States, Tennessees and Notre Dames could take a hike, because he was going to spend his college days rattling helmets in Champaign-Urbana. Word of the decision filtered out to recruiters, who shifted their attentions elsewhere. The phone at the Vasys home was suddenly ringing a lot less. Fewer coaches "just happened to be in the neighborhood." And the mailman's lumbago eased up — Arunas' mail had thinned to a tolerable level. The bird dogs had given up on their quarry.

All except Ed Krauciunas. He thought there was still a chance to interest the powerful, darkly-handsome youngster in his own alma-mater — Notre Dame. A big point in Notre Dame's favor: Krauciunas, like the Vasys family, was of Lithuanian descent. What's more, he had one of the most famous and respected names in Lithuania's athletic history.

In 1935, Krauciunas and a group of Lithuanian-American athletes had barnstormed the Baltic country in a series of exhibitions against the Lithuanian national teams. Krauciunas' sport was basketball. And he was very, very good. His uncanny talent drove the natives wild: in a game played before the country's president, he even shot — and made — free throws without looking at the hoop. ("To impress a girl in the stands," he said.) He was an instant celebrity, a hero in his homeland. The people loved Ed Krauciunas. Two years later they lionized his brother Phil, who, with the hated Adolph Hitler scowling on, led the Lithuanian national team to the European basketball championship.

So when one of the great Krauciunas brothers paid them a visit the elder Vasys' were impressed. Said Arunas: "You can't imagine how the Lithuanians respected Ed Krauciunas. My parents were really honored when he came to see us, and he made a big impression. Not long after his visit, I got the word from my mother: if I didn't go to Notre Dame I could never eat her cooking again. My mother was a good cook. I went." Ah, the wonderous ways of big-time college recruiting.

By the way, Ed Krauciunas is better known to Notre Dame fans as Ed "Moose" Krause, athletic director of the University. He only breaks out the original name to visit the homes of large Lithuanian linebackers.

★ ★ ★

Coach Hugh Devore, surveying the team in 1963: "I've got too many French poodles around here. What I need is some mad dogs."

★ ★ ★

Dismal. That was the word for the 1963 season. Hugh Devore was made interim coach, which was the University's way of saying it wanted to live with him but not get married. No commitments, please. Everyone knew that Hughie had one season to set the house in order. If he couldn't do it, the ax would come down. Only it wouldn't be the ax. They would pat him on the back and tell him the interim was up. "Interim" is one of the most beloved words in any bureaucracy.

By the final game of the season against Syracuse, Devore was as good as gone. The team had stumbled to a 2-6 record and every college coach with a readable pulse had applied for the Notre Dame job. There was this last game to play, then the hunt for a new head man would begin.

Devore wanted to go out with a win over the Orangemen. He formed his game plan carefully, and for his pre-game talk he hauled out some old-time locker room oratory. Pride — pride in Notre Dame — was at stake.

He ranted.

And he roared.

From an excited summit his voice plunged to a hoarse baritone. Rockne would have approved.

The coach crescendoed to the finish. Louder. Higher. Right up to the orgasmic phrase, "Let's get out there . . . and WIN!" . . . . when his dentures shot out of his mouth.

The pearly whites tumbled through the air. Hughie lunged and caught them before they hit the floor. But the mood was broken. Players buzzed with stifled laughter. Assistant coaches bit their cheeks.

The inadvertent slapstick was a commentary of sorts on eight years of Irish football frustrations: often it seemed they were on the brink of something good, then the fates would frown — or in Devore's case, pucker.

Notre Dame lost to Syracuse, 14-7.

★ ★ ★

Early on Christmas morning in 1962, Don Hogan, a Notre Dame sophomore and leading rusher for the 1962 football team, was involved in an auto accident on Chicago's Dan Ryan Expressway. He was injured badly. Several bones were broken and one of his hips had been cracked like a pecan shell. Never mind football, Don Hogan was going to have a tough time walking again.

But more than anything else, Hogan wanted to take the field again for Notre Dame. Miraculously, he was out for practice in the fall of 1963. But the jackhammer power, the deceptive speed, had not returned to his legs, and his comeback fell short.

Still, he followed a torturous rehabilitation program, hoping to make it back in 1964. Then in the Spring there came the agonizing realization that he was finished as a player. Don Hogan sat down and composed the following letter to his teammates:

March 16, 1964

Notre Dame Football Team:

I always felt that it was a hard job for a sportswriter to write a postmortem on an athlete who had just retired after a long sports career. But I never knew how hard it would be to write one's own.

The last thing in my mind when I registered at Notre Dame almost three years ago was that today — March 16, 1964 — I, Don Hogan, would be writing an obituary of my sports career.

It has been a long year and a half since that accident. The pressure at times has been almost unbearable. Last fall I almost made it, but then my progress halted. Over this past semester break my doctors told me I should forget about all active sports for the rest of my life. I found that ultimatum hard to take. I pleaded my case until I was given a set of exercises to try for thirty days; if they didn't do much good, all hope would be lost.

Well thirty days are up, and then some, and my condition has worsened if anything. What is my condition? The doctors tell me I have arthritis — my hip is like that of a sixty-year-old man. The reason I'm writing this letter, though, is not to tell you my condition, but to tell you why I fought so desperately to overcome it. If only each one of you could be deprived of playing ball for one year, knowing you could help the team but powerless to do anything about it.

Why did I keep trying? First of all, I wanted to play for Notre Dame; and I wanted to play with you, my fellow teammates, to be a part of you.

Being a part of Notre Dame has been the greatest and most rewarding experience of my short lifetime. When I was in the hospital I received get-well cards from people I didn't even know, from all over the country. Little kids look up to me because I'm a Notre Dame football player. I was fortunate enough to be Notre Dame's leading ground gainer, to win your respect; I'll never forget that night at the pep rally last fall when you gave me a standing ovation. But my most prized possession is that Southern California game ball you gave me. All of these things, plus thousands of people pulling for me, made me postpone my decision until all possibilities of recovery were exhausted.

I owe it to you and to my coaches to admit that my football career has ended. But I learned a great deal during my abbreviated career. I hope that all of you will learn and practice the same lesson — that is, never to give up until the game is over. By "the game" I don't mean just games on Saturday, but anything you do, whether it be a pre-spring workout or a long practice session, or anything in life for that matter — give it your all.

Being a Notre Dame football player automatically puts you in the national spotlight, more than playing for any other school. The fans will be pulling for you just as hard as they pulled for me — don't let them down. Be honest with yourself.

Well, I'd better be closing now, but I just had to tell you why I made my decision, what Notre Dame football meant to me, and what I hope it means to you. I hope that you and everyone else who has shown an interest in me will not think the less of me for making this decision.

One last thing: I'll be out there this spring and fall watching practice and your games; and if ever practice seems too long or you get tired along about that fourth quarter, just stop and think for one second that a guy named Hogan would give anything to trade places with you, and if he could he would never quit — then after you think it over give that second and third effort. Bring Notre Dame football back where it belongs. Someone in the stands will get the message of that extra effort, and that someone will be mighty pleased and proud.

Best of luck,

Don Hogan
Class of 1965

★ ★ ★

Don Hogan.

X.
Sideline People

Mr. John Campbell, a retired banker from Loudonville, New York, packs his bags every fall and checks into the University's Morris Inn for the duration of the football season.

★   ★   ★

A frail wisp of a woman who stands barely five feet tall in her orthopedic shoes, Sister Margaret Phelan from St. Mary's, has never attended a Notre Dame game in her seventy-eight years. But that doesn't mean she's not a fan. The tiny nun was a nurse in the Notre Dame infirmary for nearly thirty years, and she passes but one judgment on the football players and coaches she met there: "Wonderful."

"Each week I offer something up for a victory," she says in a soft Irish brogue. "My favorite sacrifice — because it's the hardest — is to spend the entire game in the chapel, praying. I really believe that the sisters here at St. Mary's have helped the boys win a few games over the years.

"Do I ever want to see them in person? No, not any more. In my age and condition I'd have a heart attack for certain. I'd surely be down on the field trying to run with the ball. Goodness, I get excited enough when I watch them on TV."

★   ★   ★

Bob Cahill worked for forty-eight years in the athletic department at Notre Dame, twenty-eight of them as ticket manager, which is a thankless job. Cahill was asked how he would spend a post-retirement football weekend:

"I'm going to enjoy myself. Stay up late with friends on Friday night. Go to the pre-game brunch at the Morris Inn. I'll enjoy the game and a few tailgate parties, and have a restful Sunday. Then on Monday I'll sit down at the typewriter and type a long letter to the ticket manager complaining about the lousy seats I had for the game."

★   ★   ★

Clashmore Mike was the name given to a succession of Irish terrier mascots at Notre Dame. (In recent years the mascot job has fallen to student leprechauns, who leave less of a mess on the sidelines, though they occasionally require distemper shots.) Clashmore Mike is regarded fondly by old grads, who saw the dog as the embodiment of a feisty Irish spirit.

The canine was even the subject of a book titled *Mascot Mike of Notre Dame.* The plot: clever little Mascot Mike nips and worries the Army mule during a halftime and sends the beast off humiliated. The book was one in a series on college mascots, which means that somewhere there is a book in which the Army mule drop-kicks Clashmore Mike into the Hudson River.

★   ★   ★

From Clashmore Mike we go to Terri Buck, who was anything but a dog. How many fans missed big plays during the 1970 and 1971 seasons because their binoculars were trained on the strikingly beautiful cheerleader from Connecticut?

Until Farrah Fawcett-Majors appeared at a 1974 game and caused an all-out epidemic of rubbernecking in the Notre Dame student section, Terri held the stadium single game record for male hearts set aflame.

★   ★   ★

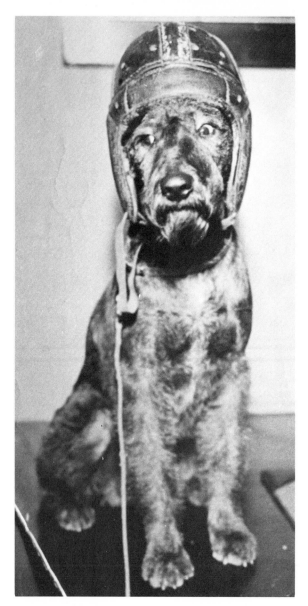

Mascot Mike fielding sportswriters' questions after a bitter loss to Purdue in 1950.

Father Bernie Lang taught the team weight-lifting for years when the coaches still scowled at the idea of pumping iron. Made the players too muscle-bound, they thought.

Lang himself was once rated the fourth strongest man in the world, and had a muscle beach figure that would have won him a walk-on part in any number of beach blanket movies. But whenever he saw one of his pupils admiring his own biceps in a mirror: BOOM! — a bop in the head; SPLASH! — into the pool. Lang felt weightlifting was for strength, not narcissism.

He was pretty ill the last few years of his life. "So weak I can barely lift three-hundred pounds," he murmured. But he remained as feisty as ever. "Let's face it," he said, "I've been a problem child all my life."

★ ★ ★

When his old pard and classmate Frank Leahy took over as head coach, Clarence ("Call me 'Kozy'") Kozak became an unofficial chaperone/gatekeeper for the team. One of his main duties was to screen the game-day visitors from the Irish locker room. After the 1945 Army game he was at his post, guarding the door to Notre Dame's Yankee Stadium dressing room. Larry McPhail — perennial hothead and boss of the Yankees — wanted in.

Clarence Kozak refused.

McPhail's face reddened. "You have to let me in," he yelped. "I own the ballpark!"

"That's too bad," said Clarence Kozak. "We rented it for the day."

Kozy still follows the Irish. Thanks to a lifetime sideline pass he gets a good view — and occasionally a good taste — of the action.

"I was down at the 1978 Cotton Bowl," he says, clipping off the words. "Right by the bench. That Texas runner — what's his name, Campbell? — he came my way. Ross Browner caught him. They both ran me over. Broke my glasses into eleven pieces. Got a big cut on my forehead. Team doctor stitched me up. Stayed right there on the field for the rest of the game."

If Kozak does not enjoy the wound he at least gets a trace of satisfaction from it: "Got a scar there," he says. "Know what I think when I feel it? Notre Dame 38, Texas 10."

★ ★ ★

There is no large music department, no opulent facility for the band at Notre Dame. The Band of the Fighting Irish draws its membership from every undergraduate major, and must work out of cramped quarters in antique Washington Hall. It remains a proud and enthusiastic organization thanks largely to one man: Robert F. O'Brien, Director of Bands.

As director since 1952, O'Brien must by now hold the collegiate record for Gershwin tunes arranged and stick men plotted (". . . and now watch our man fox-trot to the tune of 'I've Got Rhythm'").

There are at least three constants in Bob O'Brien's life: an incurable weakness for old Broadway melodies; a pair of glasses that refuse to stay on the bridge of his nose; and the loyalty and respect of two-and-a-half decades of Notre Dame bandsmen.

★ ★ ★

Since Joe Kuharich left, the loudest groans at home games have been reserved for Indiana State Police Sergeant Tim McCarthy and his traffic safety puns. McCarthy, who began the practice in 1960, found that an atrocious pun is the best way to get the crowd's attention for what is essentially a serious message. His cornball humor is now a tradition.

Are you ready? Here are Sergeant Tim's Top Five:

The automobile might have replaced the horse, but the driver should stay on the wagon.

The road may be rocky if you drive when you're stoned.

Notre Dame's leading punner.

Drive like a musician . . . C Sharp or B Flat.

Those who have one for the road may have a policeman for a chaser.

Safety first makes you last.

All together now: "Aaaaoooooooohhhhhhhhhh!"

★   ★   ★

For millions of football-thirsty Irish fans in the forties, Bill Stern meant Notre Dame football. The NBC announcer was the weekend pipeline who called the radio play-by-play in most of Notre Dame's big games. Stern was famous for his haphazard method at the mike. On certain Saturdays he would have had trouble calling a bingo.

The announcer was renowned for his "lateral play." A runner would break free on a long gainer and halfway through the play Stern would realize that he had the wrong man carrying the ball. So he invented a lateral. A fifty-yard run by Doc Blanchard when filtered through Bill Stern would come into your home as a thirty-yard run by Glenn Davis and a lateral to Blanchard, who "picked up the remaining twenty." On his worst days, Stern was like a crooked accountant: facts were juggled liberally to get the bottom line to come out right.

There were at least two occasions when he demonstrated his unique talents while covering the Irish. Into the second quarter of their 1946 opener against Illinois, Notre Dame had been stalemated. Then Emil Sitko rambled loose down the sidelines. *"Sitko with the handoff . . . he's free at the fifteen, the twenty, the thirty!"* cried Stern. Sitko's stubby legs chewed up the yard lines. A single Illinois defender blocked his path to the goal, and Jack

Zilly angled in to rub that man out. Anticipating the block, Stern's spotter pointed to Zilly's name on his chart. Bill Stern misunderstood. He thought he'd blown another one. *"Sitko laterals to Jack Zilly,"* he blurted, *"and Zilly makes a beautiful run to the Illini two-yard line!"*

The play was a biggie; it broke open the game for the Irish. Back in Southington, Connecticut, the citizenry swelled with pride. Hometown boy Jack Zilly was a hero. Their ecstasy dimmed when the Sunday paper was delivered.

But our favorite Sternism occurred the year before, at the Navy game. With the score tied 6-6 late in the final stanza the Irish surged toward paydirt in an agonizing race against the clock. On the last play of the game Boley Dancewicz was driven out of bounds at the Navy goal line. Touchdown? There was mass confusion on the field as the officials conferred.

No score, ruled the refs, to wild, arm-flapping protests from the Irish. One of the officials met with the captains at the fifty and flipped a coin to decide which team got the game ball.

The NBC audience was waiting to hear from Bill Stern, who couldn't make one whit of sense out of it all. He had to say something. Peering down at the midfield meeting, he told his listeners: *"That last call could go either way . . . . The officials are flipping a coin to see if Dancewicz got it!"*

★   ★   ★

Tudy Cummings may be the most avid follower the team has ever had. Mrs. Cummings has motored down from Chicago's south side for every home game in the last twenty-seven years, and in that time has missed only four road trips. She figures that, all told, she's seen the Irish play 475 times.

Her devotion to Notre Dame football has occasionally bordered on the fanatical. "I'm the only woman ever to take the field in a Notre Dame uniform," she says. "One spring Jack Leahy, who was a student manager, snuck me into the dressing room. I put on a uniform and ran onto the field, and some players who were there chased me and tackled me.

"Also, my husband and I honeymooned in Cleveland."

Cleveland?

"Notre Dame and Navy were playing there that weekend."

Fans may come, fans may go. But Tudy Cummings takes the prize. There is nothing more fanatical than a honeymoon in Cleveland.

★   ★   ★

XI.

Not a Bandwagon Big Enough

1964-1974

Not long after Ara Parseghian was hired, Moose Krause got a call from an angry alumnus. "Moose, what the hell's going on up there?" he stormed. "This guy's not a Notre Dame man, and he's a Presbyterian to boot! I stayed with 'em when they were down, but this is the last straw. This Parcheesian or whatever his name is doesn't get my support."

Krause could not placate the man.

Eight months later, when the Irish were in the midst of the 1964 revival, the alumnus called again. "Moose, I thought I'd let you know I'm back on the bandwagon," he said. "I think Ara and the boys are doing a bang-up job. Guess it doesn't make any difference if he's a non-Catholic."

"Of course not," said Krause. "Why, Rockne himself was at Notre Dame for twenty years before he became a Catholic."

"So you think Ara will convert?"

"Listen," confided the athletic director, "if he keeps winning he'll convert. He'll convert all of us to Presbyterians."

★   ★   ★

So by the end of the 1964 season, Ara Parseghian's relationship with Notre Dame was just hunky-dory. There wasn't a bandwagon big enough for all his supporters. But there had been a bit of choppy water in the beginning: a few alumni, like the one above, wanted a bedrock Catholic as coach; and there was a conflict of unknown origin that caused Ara to change his mind — briefly — about wanting the job in the first place.

On December 16, 1963, Notre Dame had scheduled a press conference in the Morris Inn to announce The Hiring. Thirty members of the press gathered in a conference room while Parseghian and Father Joyce, vice-president in control of athletics, met in an upstairs suite. The press waited. And waited. It soon became evident that something was amiss. Hugh Devore, who had been in the room to brief the reporters, glanced nervously at his watch, loosened his tie, made frequent trips to the bathroom — he was stalling for time.

Two hours behind schedule, Parseghian showed. Quite obviously, he was angry. He paused in the lobby of the hotel, read a terse statement saying he had not yet decided to take the job, then stalked out to his car and gunned it toward Chicago.

A swarm of reporters buzzed around Father Joyce, whose only comment was: "No comment." Moose Krause said the same.

The reporters suddenly found themselves with a story that had twisted beyond recognition; they scrambled to find the reason for Parseghian's puzzling change of mind. One fellow fished through wastebaskets until he found the scrap of paper on which the coach had written his statement. Another chased Joyce to his office and shouted at him over the office intercom until the priest emerged, just as tight-lipped as before. Still others, in the finest journalistic tradition, retired to the Morris Inn bar for the afternoon. There was much speculation, but no one ever learned the subject of the disagreement.

Whatever it was, it made no difference, because Ara and Joyce settled the conflict after a couple of days. Notre Dame had their coach. The high-voltage electricity that had been but back since the days of Leahy was flowing again — thanks to a Presbyterian Armenian with jet black hair and drop-forged eyes.

The reason Parseghian walked out of the press conference? Fifteen years later, the people who know still aren't talking. Even insiders in the administration can't find out: "Goodness knows, I've tried," says a high-ranking priest. "I even played it cagey. I waited for a couple of years, then asked Ara about it in an offhand way. No dice."

Father Joyce and Parseghian pledged to keep the disagreement a secret. Not even Bill Cullen, Kitty Carlisle, Tom Poston and Peggy Cass could crack that one.

★   ★   ★

Why is Norm Nicola smiling? Perhaps because he was named to a national All-Italian team even though he was Lebanese.

★   ★   ★

No sooner did Parseghian become coach than Sports Information Director Charlie Callahan got a call from his opposite number at Purdue.

"Okay, Charlie," said the Boilermaker SID, "spell it for me."

"Easy," answered Callahan. "P-a-r-s-e-g-h-i-a-n."

"Naw, I want to see if you've learned how to spell Presbyterian."

★ ★ ★

The wave started slowly: from Tom Swifties and elephant jokes to biting political satire; from AuH_2O to the Great Society; from Beatlemania to Flower Power.

It rose: *All in the Family;* Robert McNamara: moon shots and "marihuana;" Louise Day Hicks and Stokley Carmichal.

It peaked: Nixon and Agnew, Kent State, Woodstock, Vietnam, peace rallies and draft dodgers and a country split down the seams.

It disintegrated: Henry Kissinger; Peter Rodino and John Dean; Altamont, Jesus freaks, *Helter-Skelter.*

This was no easy ride, especially not for a football coach. It was no longer enough to give a player a quick pep talk and a slap on the butt. Everything had to be [a favorite term] "relevant." And the sacrifices that a coach had once expected as a matter of form were rejected by many players as too confining, conforming, and contemptible.

Ara Parseghian rode the wave better than most. His record was 95-17-4. The respect he had from players and fans and alumni when he walked away from the job in 1974 was even higher than that.

★ ★ ★

Friday nights before home games have been the

same for years. After the pep rally, the team repairs to Moreau Seminary, just across St. Joseph's Lake from the campus. A movie is screened in the seminary auditorium; apples and oranges laid out for snacks. Then it's upstairs into the guest rooms (a drastic drop in projected vocations always ensures plenty of empty cubicles) and lights are off within half an hour.

In 1964, Ara Parseghian's taste in movies ran mostly to John Wayne shoot-'em-ups, innocuous fare to ease the pressure the team was sure to feel each Friday night. But Ara took one occasion to make sure his team was not too relaxed. It was October 23, 1964, the eve of the Stanford game.

When John Wayne finally kissed his horse good-bye and the Friday night flick faded away, the team stirred, and began to get up to hit the hay.

"Sit down." Parseghian was curt.

The team sat. The lights stayed out and another film lit the screen. At first it looked like bad black-and-white home movies. The team stared, then gulped and grimaced, recognizing scenes from the 1963 debacle that ended in a 24-14 upset for Stanford. Not one word was said as the film flickered on. There was Huarte getting sacked, dropping the ball; the defense swinging open like a barn door; Irish runners tripping, falling, being tackled behind the lines. Mercifully it ended in fifteen minutes.

"Now," said Parseghian, "go up and sleep on that."

The next day it was midway through the third quarter before Stanford got their initial first down. The Irish had another win on the way to an apparent national championship.

★ ★ ★

Notre Dame and Southern Cal have been

settling some sort of grudge since pigs were used for footballs. And never were the Irish in a more vengeful mood than when USC came to town in 1965. The year before, Notre Dame's national championship dreams had gone up in a puff of Los Angeles smog when the Trojans stole the game in the final seconds. Irish fans rushed to their calendars to mark the ten months, twenty-five days, and eighteen hours until the teams met again.

The day of the 1965 meeting was misty, wind-swept and altogether grey. Southern Cal Coach John McKay had seen that kind of South Bend weather before. But he had never weathered a crowd like that one. "Remember" and "Revenge!" buttons dotted the stadium like a mad mosaic. Even before the game began, the crowd was on its feet, howling. Noise cascaded from all sides, making the field the eye of a hurricane of sound.

The roar peaked as Ken Ivan kicked off for the Irish. USC's Mike Hunter waited to receive the kick. He caught the ball — then fell flat on his face.

John McKay looked on in consternation. "My God," he shouted, eyeing the frenzied partisans in the stands, "they've *shot* him!"

When you're a Hatfield you come to expect anything from the McCoys.

★ ★ ★

Jack Robinson knew a good bet when he saw it. The captain of the 1934 team, Robinson, who had since had both legs amputated because of a circulatory disorder, came back to South Bend in 1965 to watch the Iowa game, which was played in a blizzard. "I'll give anyone odds that I'm the only person in the stadium wearing Bermuda shorts," he said.

★ ★ ★

Nearly every young athlete has an idol, and Mike Burgener's was Tommy McDonald, an All-Pro receiver with the Eagles. Burgener was as small as McDonald, and he tried to be as gritty, as tough. He emulated McDonald in every way he could.

Yearly, the managers ask each player to specify the type of face mask he wants on his helmet. Burgener, in his first varsity year, opted for a mask like his idol's: a single bar tilted at a low angle, leaving the face almost fully exposed.

Burgener's varsity baptism came on the kick-off team. He lined up, and with the kick of the ball flew down the field in a hell-bent kamikaze attack on the runner. But a big forearm sledge-hammered into his unprotected face. Blood streaming, his nose in a new attitude, Burgener staggered to the bench and

grabbed a student manager. He tapped on the Tommy McDonald face mask. "Any chance of getting this replaced before the next kick-off?" he asked.

Everyone's loyalty has its limits . . . .

★ ★ ★

"It got to the point," says Ara Parseghian, "where it was ridiculous."

Ara's reference is to the attention given the 1966 Michigan State game. "To accomodate the media I had to hold press conferences before and after each practice," he says. "There's not much you can say that's newsworthy about a practice. But I had to relate in minute detail everything we did. Right down to whose jockstrap had snapped."

The hoopla surrounding game week strung out players from both teams to an incredible tension. Fans and press made it clear that it was the battle of the decade, if not the century. Eighteen year-olds can get pretty skittish under that kind of pressure.

After the Wednesday evening meal Parseghian asked the team to listen to what he claimed was a tape of five Michigan State players in a radio interview. The team listened to the Spartans, who belittled the Irish. General astonishment swept the room.

Then there was laughter, as the squad realized that "five MSU players" were one person: Tom Pagna, the offensive backfield coach. Under five aliases, Pagna blustered brashly about the Spartans' chances. In a tense week, it was a relaxing moment. Jaws that hadn't been unclenched for days loosened into smiles.

And then the game. What can you say about it? It was a 10-10 tie, and Notre Dame sat on the ball in the dying seconds, and Michigan State considered this a cowardly thing to do, and never the twain

Michigan State's Duffy Daugherty offers his opinion of the 1966 10-10 tie.

shall meet. But what players and coaches remember about the game is the craziness on the sidelines.

"The Michigan State band was right behind us. I don't think they ever quit playing. Between them and the crowd I was numb with the noise," says one Notre Damer.

"There were people — just regular fans — sitting on the team bench. I couldn't believe it," says another.

"What had happened," reflects Parseghian, "is that everyone and his brother who had favors coming asked for tickets. There just weren't enough seats in the stadium, so the schools gave out sideline passes — over a thousand of them. If I wanted to get to our bench to see an injured player I

Mike Burgener — after the crunch.

A blimp's eye view of Notre Dame Stadium. The double-domed Athletic and Convocation Center squats directly across Juniper Road.

had to literally fight through the fans.

"I remember once I was trying to watch a third-down play. I start to move up the sideline and there, right next to me, is a man I'd never seen before. This guy is wearing a big fur coat and smoking a cigar. I said, 'What the hell are you doing here?'"

"He said, 'Same thing you are, coach. I'm watching the game.'"

★ ★ ★

Though strict campus regulations were beginning to ease a bit, cars were still prohibited for everybody but seniors. Bicycling was the most popular, indeed, the only means of underclass transportation. And, reflecting the tenor of the times, all the bikes had locks. All, that is, but one. That bicycle had "A. PAGE" printed plainly on the seat; no one ever thought of touching it.

Alan Page, later NFL Most Valuable Player.

★ ★ ★

Goeddeke.

From his first day at Notre Dame, George Goeddeke sported a shaved head, a striking sight midst the crew cuts and Hollywood burrs affected by most students. A few years later, when England's mop-topped Beatles created the shaggy hair boom and put barbers out of business all over the country, Goeddeke's shiny dome stuck out like the cue ball on a pool table. Still, who's going to point a finger and snicker at a six-foot three-inch, two-hundred thirty-pound center? Not us.

The bald head became Goeddeke's trademark. "Mr. Clean," he was dubbed; he was so enchanted with the image that he arrived at school one fall wearing an earring, just like his namesake on the detergent bottle. When he did let his hair grow, it was to achieve a special effect — such as the time he saluted the American Indian by growing a swatch down the middle of his head, Mohawk style; or the time he celebrated St. Patrick's Day by shaving a patch of hair in the shape of a shamrock and dying it green.

What went on under George's head was as utterly non-conformist. Notre Dame's off-center center expressed his individualism even in the vehicles he drove, and where he drove them. In the fall of his senior year, he showed up behind the wheel of a used hearse he had purchased during the summer. "I gotta good deal on it," he assured classmates. "The undertaker is a personal friend of mine."

On one occasion, Goeddeke and a buddy decided to ride their motorcycles through O'Shaughnessy Hall, the long liberal arts building at the south end of campus that Frank Lloyd Wright once called "the world's biggest men's room." The two easy riders wheeled their mammoth machines into the building, gunned the engines deafeningly, and roared down the hall past twenty classrooms, prompting several of the more sensitive professorial types into an early retirement.

During the 1966 season, Goeddeke was lacing up his shoes for practice when he overheard some teammates marvelling at Parseghian's stubbornly strict, almost military drilling procedures. On certain days, they noted, Ara never allowed himself to come down from the tower from which he directed practice. Goeddeke, an avowed enemy of the status quo, made a characteristic boast: "I bet I can get him down from there."

No way, the others argued. Ara's timetable for week-day workouts was so precise that he didn't allow himself a sneeze if he hadn't allotted time for it. Bringing him off the tower? Impossible.

That afternoon, midway through a full contact scrimmage, Goeddeke got hit and fell to the turf groaning in pain. Worried teammates, trainers, and assistants hovered over the now motionless super center, trying to diagnose the injury. "Better not move him," someone suggested. "It may be his back." Bare heads and helmets nodded in grim accord.

By this time — believe it or not — Ara had climbed down from the tower to check on the situation. He stared down at Goeddeke. "What's wrong with him?" he asked anxiously.

Goeddeke rolled over. "Nothing, Coach," he said with the hint of a grin. "I just wanted to see if you cared."

★   ★   ★

USC coach John McKay, to his team after it had absorbed a 51-0 shellacking at the hands of the Fighting Irish: "Forget it guys. Do you realize there are 700 million Chinese who don't even know the game was played?"

★   ★   ★

The young men who populate the prep teams must wonder at times why they go through with it.

A coach hands you a ball and designates you Bob Griese of Purdue. You know for a fact that you can't throw that ball like Bob Griese, and you have serious doubts that your line will protect you like Griese's line protects him. But that doesn't alter the frightful vision of a ton and a half of varsity defense waiting across the line, stomping and snorting and growling, *imagining* that you're Bob Griese, and painting a mental bullseye on your sternum. It can be a long season.

That's why, when the preppers have had an especially brutal year they throw a banquet for themselves. A licking of the wounds. Appetizers, main course and dessert consist mainly of beer — several cubic yards of it, downed with great enthusiasm. Then there's the highlight of the evening: crowning of the Least Valuable Player.

To choose the LVP the preppers view a practice scrimmage film and vote on the player least talented at his position. Competition is keen. There are always a boat-load of preppers who are genuinely rotten; the problem is to narrow the choice to a single inept individual.

One year a cornerback (whom we'll call Digby) had tossed down a good many brews and was lobbying loudly for the award: "I should get it," he argued. "There's no one who means less to this team than I do. You've heard of guys who can do it all? — well, I can't do any of it. Without me, Notre Dame might have been the national champion!"

But the film was the final judge. Midway through the showing Digby flashed onto the screen. He had the perfect angle to tackle Nick Eddy along the sideline. Eddy dipped a shoulder. Digby spun around and fell like a man who'd just had his ankles yanked by a rope. He didn't lay a hand on the runner.

"Digby!" cried the preppers when the film had ended. "Digby's got it!" There was general consensus that his play on Eddy was one of the worst ever captured on film.

"Just a second." The speaker was a pale sophomore in the rear of the room. "Is there anyone here who didn't get into that scrimmage?"

Silence.

"That makes me the Least Valuable Player," he said. "I didn't get in. I must be the worst."

The logic was airtight. Unanimously, the soph was chosen LVP.

★   ★   ★

When Joe Freebery crumpled to the ground, everyone knew it was no prank. Football can be a tough business, wrapping the head in a plastic bubble, then demanding wind sprints, crab walks and sled drills from the body. On a sweltering, ninety-degree September day, this regimen can devour the best of athletes. It almost killed Joe Freebery.

As soon as he went down, cries for help split the air; practice skidded to a halt. Dr. George Colip and team trainer Gene Paszkiet rushed to the fallen linebacker. A split-second inspection by Colip revealed one alarming fact: Freebery's heart had stopped beating.

Paszkiet and Colip had only minutes to save a man's life or watch it slip away. They fell to their task like a well-trained team, two men working as one performing cardiopulmonary resuscitation. Paszkiet pried open the air passage to the lungs and sent bursts of breath down with periodic mouth-to-mouth resuscitation. Colip attempted to stimulate the heart by pounding Freebery's chest with the side of his fist. Something had to work, and quickly: the continuous exchange of oxygen, the hard, sharp smacking of the sternum. Finally, miraculously, there was a heartbeat and breathing. Freebery awoke. He remembered nothing. He seemed to be all right.

Then he collapsed again. This time Colip and Paszkiet were able to keep him conscious until a hospital ambulance arrived. Freebery's condition was later diagnosed as pericarditis, a dangerous and often fatal inflammation of the heart's surrounding membrane. Happily, he recovered beautifully; he was back at practice a year later and playing once more.

There is absolutely no doubt that Gene Paszkiet and Doctor Colip saved Joe Freebery's life. It does no good to complain that behind-the-scenes men like these do not get the publicity they deserve. They never have and never will, because they don't chart plays or wear headphones or banter with reporters at post-game press conferences. But at times like that sweltering September afternoon, their job is much more satisfying, infinitely more important. Ask Joe Freebery.

★　★　★

Ron Dushney, a halfback on the 1966, 1967 and 1968 teams, made this observation during a blistering hot practice session: "You know, hard work is not easy."

★　★　★

Fully outfitted for practice, Dennis Kiliany looked like a man on his way to defuse a bomb. From his fingers to his toes, Kiliany would be encased in every conceivable type of padding. Knuckle pads. Forearm pads. Upper arm pads. Rib pads . . . . Styrofoam stock would jump six points when Dennis Kiliany took the field.

To this day, equipment manager Gene O'Neill gives an award to the player showing the most imaginative style with his uniform. "We call it the Denny Kiliany Award," says O'Neill.

★　★　★

Who has not joined the light, scattered applause that follows the lowliest benchwarmer onto the field for a brief taste of glory? Granted, reserves almost never get into a game that has been in doubt for less than a month. Still, you have to feel a little jolt of joy for the guy who's finally playing in a real game against a real opponent.

Which brings us to a grey, windy, freezing day at Philadelphia's JFK Stadium. Over the years, thousands of Philadelphians have moved to Florida and Arizona, and all because of days like this. Up in the stands, people were checking their fingers for frostbite. Down on the field, Notre Dame was dancing the expected jig over a hapless Navy bunch. The lead was insurmountable midway through the fourth quarter, and anxious glances were being exchanged at the far corner of the Irish bench. Four reserves were worried: Ara would be sending them into the game very soon.

Hours earlier, long before the kick-off, these four had trotted onto the field for a few calistentics, a few run-through plays. Then they spent the rest of the afternoon frozen to the bench. Numbed to the bone, all four were wondering if they could move well enough to lumber back to the locker room at game's end. Now it seemed they would have to enter that beastly, dangerous swirl of blocking and tackling and protect themselves against serious injury.

A big tackle tried to warm up by swinging his arms and found he was moving with the agility of a sedated hippo.

Another man discovered he could not feel his legs. "How can I run?" he whined, his shoulder pads chattering softly as he shivered.

A third remained grimly silent, hot breath steaming through his face mask. Uneasily, he pictured his brittle body getting dashed to a field as hard as a hockey rink.

A fourth string scatback wrapped words around it: "We could get killed!"

The assistant coaches were coldly scanning the bench now, preparing to put fresh blood into the center of the arena. The four reserves averted their eyes. In doing so, they noticed the cloaks.

Wide were these cloaks and thick, made to wrap

around the most gigantic, heavily padded football monsters. All the extras were there, heaped in a huge pile just to the left and slightly behind the four reserves.

The idea sparked in every brain; it beckoned like a warming bonfire.

The halfback looked appealingly at the tackle. "Nah," quivered the big fellow. "We couldn't."

The players stared back out to the field. The first-stringers, the stars, were out there, getting their pictures snapped. They would know delights the reserves could only imagine: fan letters, pro offers, and girls with perfect teeth.

The reserves considered that. They compared their plight: so many years on the bench, bottled up, dusty, unused. All those Saturdays spent cheering for the first-string glamour boys.

Now the reserves were supposed to enter this freezing, dangerous contest, at great risk, and give the first team a head start toward the warmth of the dressing room. Two of the reserves glanced back at the cloaks; the other two checked the coaches, who were already beginning wholesale substitution.

"To hell with it," said one. "Let's do it."

All silently agreed.

Smoothly, quietly, hardly betraying their stiffness, the four slunk off the bench and crawled under the cloaks. When the assistants came looking for them, the four reserves were safe and warm and well-hidden. Their chance to play had finally come. They didn't want it.

★ ★ ★

A large map of the United States and its territories hung in Ara's office. Wide, impressive-looking lines were drawn all over the map, charting out each coach's recruiting responsibilities. Ara's

own far-flung territories were clearly marked: Hawaii and the Virgin Islands.

There are certain advantages to being the head coach . . . .

★ ★ ★

Nearest anyone could guess, Leon Hart Jr. was about six-foot eight, about 280 pounds — far and away the largest fellow reporting for the freshman team in the fall of 1970. But he was never dressed for practice. He seemed healthy enough, but while the team suffered the two-a-day tortures of fall drills, Leon Jr. stood on the sidelines in sweat clothes. Speculation was rife: why wasn't this young behemoth in uniform?

He wasn't dressed because Notre Dame didn't have a helmet to fit him. In fact, no one in the country had a helmet to fit him. Before he could suit up, Leon had to wait until a sporting goods company built a bonnet big enough for his size eight-and-a-half head.

★ ★ ★

First came the attack in the humid night when the North Vietnamese bullet ripped through Robert "Rocky" Bleier's left leg. Then, moments later, a grenade bounced toward him and detonated, shooting its wicked shards of metal into his legs and feet, inflicting wounds that ended his tour of duty in Vietnam.

Bleier had been a three year letterman at halfback for Notre Dame and captain of the 1967 squad. When his draft notice came in the mail he was in training camp with the Pittsburgh Steelers in the summer of 1968. A few months later he was hauling a grenade launcher through a jungle thousands of miles from pro football. After his

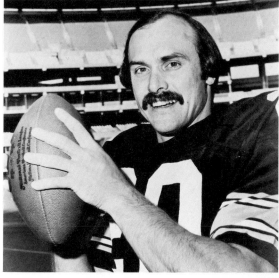

Rocky

wounds he was even farther from the game. A comeback, almost everyone advised him, was an unreachable goal.

But something other than the deeply embedded shrapnel remained with Rocky Bleier, as one of his former teammates observed: "I was a freshman when he was a senior. He was the guy I really looked up to, tried to pattern myself after. To me, he was the ideal team captain. Here he was back for a pep rally in 1969, thirty pounds under his playing weight, walking with a bad limp — he didn't even look like the guy I remembered. But when he spoke he had that same spirit, that same fire in him. Listening to him speak at that rally was the most moving experience I had at Notre Dame."

Quite simply, the man refused to quit on himself. He hobbled back into the Steeler's training camp in 1970, and after two arduous years of fighting his way through waivers, injury lists, and taxi squads,

Rocky was back. His gritty play characterized the style of a Steeler team that won its first championship in forty years. By 1975 he was a Super Bowl Champion.

★ ★ ★

Great economist, bad geographer.

Reggie Barnett's remarkable intellect was never in doubt. The Flint, Michigan, native was at least as brilliant in the classroom as on the football field. A cornerback who covered fiscal policy as well as fly patterns, he graduated in 1975 with a 3.5 average in Economics. He needed only six credit-hours for a Masters degree.

But a freshman is a freshman, no matter how fast he whisks through Calculus 125 or the forty-yard dash. When Barnett arrived at Notre Dame in the fall of 1971 he was, heart and soul, a first-year man, cut from the same wide-eyed, gullible bolt of cloth as his 1,600 classmates.

He had to adapt.

Only he had to do it more quickly than most, because through some quirk of the University housing office he was assigned to a room in Sorin Hall with five socially precocious sophomores. The room, identified by a sign over the door as "The Mangy Moose Saloon," was decorated in garish shades of red, white and blue. Desks had been removed to make room for a commercial-size bar. There were black lights everywhere. Barnett had expected a dormitory and was getting a discotheque. He probably wondered if he was supposed to trade in his slide rule for a swizzle stick. The arrangement was unsettling for a sober seventeen-year-old.

Improbably, the freshman and his roommates got along well — though he did get an occasional jab when his guard was down.

Reggie was in his room in the fall of 1971, packing a suitcase for a trip to Mexico City, where the Irish frosh were to play a team of Mexican All-Stars. Tim Demarais, one of his roommates, sauntered in. When he learned Barnett's destination, he was struck with an idea.

He slipped away to an outside phone. Then in a camaflouged voice he called the freshman,

introduced himself as a football manager, and told of a freak six-inch snowfall in Mexico City. "They're expecting a lot more," Demarais said. "I'm supposed to call everyone on the team and tell them to pack winter clothes."

Barnett panicked. He shoveled out knit shirts, replaced them with sweaters, and hurriedly scoured his locker for warmer clothes. Demarais and a couple of the sophomores strolled in casually to watch.

"It's snowing in Mexico!" Barnett panted. "I need to borrow some boots."

"You can have mine," a roommate volunteered. "Do you want my skis?"

Reggie looked up. "I didn't know they had mountains in Mexico City," he said.

"They don't," was the reply. "We were trying to put one over on you."

"That's what I figured," yukked the victim, as he pulled on a big green parka. "I'm catching onto your act."

Repacked, Barnett did indeed look like he was going south — to join Admiral Byrd. Snowshoes and a team of Huskies would have topped off his ensemble. There were more sweaters in his suitcase than in all of Mexico. "You're all set," nodded the sophs.

The freshman waddled to the bus stop. A few of his teammates were already there, and he saw immediately that something was amiss: they were lightly clad in jackets and sports shirts; he was the only one who looked like an Afro-American Eskimo. "But the snow! . . ." he groaned, halfway realizing what had happened. Someone had to tell him that it hadn't snowed in Mexico City since reptiles ruled the earth.

Barnett dashed. Back to the Mangy Moose, where he repacked to generous applause from his roommates, and out again to the bus stop, where he barely caught his ride to the airport.

It was the wrong day to ask Reggie Barnett his opinion of college sophomores.

★   ★   ★

There are two ways for an offensive tackle to clear out his area of the defensive line: play clean or play dirty. No one was dirtier than Dennis Lozzi, at least for one play.

JV game; Notre Dame twelve yards from paydirt; fourth and one. The Irish decide to try a quarterback sneak. It's Lozzi's job to clear that extra foot up front so Notre Dame can hold onto the ball.

Lozzi.

Lozzi bends over and takes his position. Jams his fingers into the moist sod. It's clammy inside this helmet, he thinks. Now he sucks in his breath; he hears the signals. Lozzi feels nervous. No, wait, he feels sick. At the hike Lozzi snaps forward and throws up at the same time. Not just a bit; lots, and in all directions. The defense retreats like movie extras fleeing a Hollywood monster. The Notre Dame quarterback, displaying uncommon courage, picks his way through for a score. There isn't a defender within twenty feet of him.

Thank you, Dennis Lozzi. You gave it your all. Or at least you gave it your lunch.

★   ★   ★

Ara Parseghian, during a banquet speech: "As a crutch to help emcees remember my name, I used to tell them it was 'par,' like the golf score, 'seeg,' like the first half of Seagrams, and 'yen,' like the Japanese coin. But it didn't help. I kept getting introduced as a drunken Japanese golfer."

★   ★   ★

Dave Casper swears it's the only time he ever counselled a teammate. "Let it roll off your back like water off a duck," he told Eric Penick, who had been letting the coaches' daily carping get to him. "Coaches yell for the sake of yelling. They don't mean anything by it. Next time they get on you, just think of yourself as a duck; let it roll off your back."

Thereafter, Penick's ritual, though it served a serious purpose, would break up a practice. Every time a coach harangued him Eric would hunch up his shoulders, point his feet at Chaplinesque angles, and waddle back to the huddle sounding off like a mallard: "Quack, quack! Quack, quack!"

★   ★   ★

Stressing a point, Bill Hickey style.

Bill Hickey was everything you'd ever want in a Notre Dame assistant — and more. His hair was cropped short, as were his pants. (He wore short pants to practice no matter what the weather.) He ran five miles every day, and kept himself in a physical trim that made the Marines look like hairdressers on holiday. His sons, God bless 'em, were named Timothy Rockne and Patrick Leahy. If there was ever a man with a destiny it was Bill Hickey. He was meant to coach the Fighting Irish.

Though his position as freshman coordinator and coach of the prep team defense was not high on the staff totem pole, Hickey labored enthusiastically. He loved to see his preppers stop the varsity, and would employ all sorts of stratagems to that end. One afternoon the preppers, using a mixed bag of line stunts and blitzes, walled off the first-team offense for ten straight plays. Parseghian blew up. *"Dammit, Hickey,"* he howled, slamming a notebook to the ground, "cut that out!"

But usually the varsity stomped on the prep team, a frustrating sight for Coach Hickey, who often got so antsy that he'd thunder in and make a tackle or two himself.

In a 1972 scrimmage Willie Townsend took an end-around unmolested for a touchdown. As Townsend trotted across the end zone he failed to notice a fire-breathing Bill Hickey racing after him. Hickey zeroed in for the kill; Willie kept trotting.

From five yards away, Hickey leaped.

Townsend stopped.

Arms flailing, Hickey flew past his bemused target and tumbled headlong into a double-somersault. Give it a 9.5, 9.5, 9.3, 9.4, and a 6.0 from the East German judge.

At that instant the horn signalling the end of practice sounded. Destiny's hyperactive child hopped and jogged to the dressing room. It was all in a day's work.

★　★　★

The usher ducked as an orange whizzed by his ear. In celebration of the team's 1972 bowl bid the students were firing hundreds of oranges onto the playing field. But some of the weaker arms were pelting cheerleaders with their tosses. And lucky spectators were getting zapped in the backs of their heads. "Going to the Cotton Bowl would be safer," remarked the usher as another piece of fruit splattered into the first row seats, "but I'm thankful

we're not going to the Gator Bowl."

★　★　★

No doubt about it. The 1973 Orange Bowl was not a bad case of delirium tremens from the New Year's Eve night before. It's in the record book and it says 40-6, Nebraska over Notre Dame. Now it's coming back to you, right? There's Johnny Rodgers running wild — scoring, scoring, scoring — a stark contrast to the complete collapse of the Irish offense. Hemmed in by that quick Cornhusker "D", Notre Dame's runners were unable to break loose all evening. That's not to say that the Irish backfield spent the entire two weeks in Miami without showing some good moves. Halfbacks Art Best and Eric Penick were brilliant in the Orange Bowl Parade.

Two nights before the game, the team was bused down to a Collins Avenue reviewing stand, choice parade positions, but not good enough for Best and Penick. These two immediately snided off and mingled with some participants who were forming up to begin the march. One float especially intrigued them: a Walt Disney job ringed with children bouncing big balloons. Here, thought Best and Penick, are people we can relate to.

Some pleasant bantering with the kids sparked an idea. The Irish backs found a parade official, introduced themselves, and asked if they might join in the festivities. "No problem," said the official, a nice man with an eye for the absurd.

Approximately half an hour later, the section of the reviewing stand containing the Notre Dame team first rippled, then exploded with laughter as the Walt Disney float approached. There were Best and Penick, the blithe spirits of Notre Dame backfield, dribbling balloons and waving to the crowd right along with their ten year-old

companions. Those fellows skipped to the beat of a decidedly different drummer.

★　★　★

Dave Casper, in what may be the most damning testimony ever against the team's training table food: "I would've rather eaten at Taco Bell."

★　★　★

There are good psych jobs and there are bad psych jobs. Al Conover couldn't have psyched a cat into chasing a mouse.

As the Rice coach in 1973, Conover announced that his home game with Notre Dame would be a special "Father's Day." And when the evening of the game rolled around, there were over one hundred Catholic priests ("Fathers," get it?) assembled behind the Rice bench. Seventeen purported Catholics from the Owls were named co-captains and trotted out to mid-field for the toss of the coin.

The Rice band got into the spirit of things by forming a lemon on the field and saluting the Notre Dame team with a limp version of "I Can See Clearly Now." Droll, very droll. The PA announcer lisped a sarcastic tribute to Knute Rockne: "Imagine being there in the locker room," his voice echoed; "the sights, the sounds, the *stink* of the locker room . . . the band will play *Clean Up, America."*

The on-field antics made Conover's locker room pep talk all the easier. He didn't even have to throw a chair through a window — a little trick he had employed the year before with great success. Whatever he said, it worked. His players carried the negative charge onto the field. One fellow was so wired that he spit in Reggie Barnett's face after a play.

What does any of this — the irrelevant religious muck, the insults, the unbridled emotions — have to do with winning a football game? Not much. The Owls were pasted with a 28-0 whitewash. As for Conover? God only knows what kind of stunts he could pull on a Mother's Day.

★ ★ ★

Offensive Line Coach Wally Moore stopped the projector and loudly, vigorously, addressed his charges. "There, there, that's what I like to see." Moore was standing up now, pointing to the frozen image on the screen. "Good, clean, sharp blocking." Moore was walking to the front of the room. "Look at those blocks." He was ecstatic. "All along the line, beautiful, beautiful!" Moore was standing before the screen, his chubby face glowing in the light of the projector; he was off again on another of his innumerable blustery pep talks.

"Do you know what we'd have with guys doing that all the time? Clapping hands and *charging* out of the huddle?" Moore swatted his palms together. He was excited now, leaning forward like a bird about to take flight. "Do you know what we'd have? With enthusiasm? With toughness? Everyone driving through on his block? A sharp looking team? A hard playing team? Do you know what we'd have?"

Moore stared, wild-eyed, at the players.

The players blinked back.

The silence was excruciating.

Moore knew he had to say something.

"We'd have," he finally shouted, "a bunch of *Fighting Bastards!*"

At which the whole team broke out laughing.

★

His psych job differed slightly before the 1966 freshman game against Michigan State. That battle was scheduled one day before the "Game of the Decade" between the MSU and Notre Dame varsity teams. Moore was, predictably, swept up in the tension and excitement that had swirled round the Notre Dame coaching staff all week. He intended to transfer some of that energy to his freshman charges as they sat there in the East Lansing locker room.

Moore opened his mouth. No words.

He moved his arms. No words.

He strained, red-faced, popping muscles in his neck and rolling his eyes. No words.

Wally Moore was so excited he could not speak, making this the first pep talk in pantomime.

★

The only other derailment of the Wally Moore non-stop pep talk express came three days before the 1973 USC game. Moore was standing tip-toe on the practice field, haranguing the wind-sprinting offensive line. Suddenly, he stopped in mid-pep.

"Oh, my God," he cried. "It's a UFO!"

Six players skidded to a halt and peered anxiously into the sky.

There was the Goodyear blimp.

★ ★ ★

Eric Penick, recounting his mental state for the 1973 victory over Southern Cal: "I was psyched up when I went on the field and I'm still psyched. I'll probably be psyched till the day I die."

★ ★ ★

Eric Penick is still psyched.

When Bob Thomas was beseiged by reporters in the dressing room after his game-winning kick in the Sugar Bowl he told them that the 23-yarder had been ". . . no different from any other kick. I didn't spend time thinking about it; I just kicked it." A nice, wholesome reply. But pretty much a stock-in trade remark for athletes who have performed under pressure.

Scoreboard lights . . .

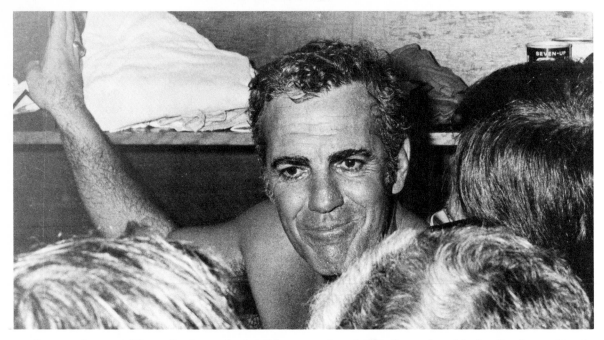

. . . lit an unforgettable smile, brought Ara his second national championship in the Sugar Bowl.

Come on, Bob. What's it really like, standing out there by your lonesome on a slippery pad of Polyturf, waiting to put your instep to a ball whose flight will decide the national championship, while 80,000 fans scream and millions watch on national TV? Says Thomas: "You can ask our equipment manager, Gene O'Neill. He's the one who had to clean my game pants."

★ ★ ★

Joe Pszeracki was never a headliner on the football field. But every year at Rookie Night, when freshmen get up and perform outlandish burlesque for the coaches and team, Joe Pszeracki was the feature show.

To be sure, there have been some memorable performances: Tom Parise's impersonation of Parseghian was a big hit; Eric Penick shaved his head and did an Isaac Hayes number that laid them in the aisles. But after freshmen and other amateurs had had their say, it was time to get down to some serious show business. The call would go out for Pszeracki.

He would only take the stage with great reluctance, but once he got there it was strictly showtime. He'd rip off his shirt to reveal the most massive pectoral (chest) muscles on the team. Cheers from the crowd.

Someone would clap his hands and begin to sing the Fight Song. Pszeracki's big pectorals would go into their act. He'd flex them in time to the music and the crowd would go wild. Blip, bloop. Right, left. They looked like two rabbits dancing just below the surface of his skin. It was stage presence! Charisma! Before long everyone in the auditorium was clapping and singing along.

When the Fight Song ended, Joe would do requests. He could twitch in time to anything.

★   ★   ★

Tom Clements: not completely in control.

The chest master.

For the umpteenth week of their careers Tom Clements and Frank Allocco were sitting with Parseghian, rehearsing his elaborate code for signalling plays from the sidelines. Part of Ara's coaching philosophy was his insistence on calling every play from the bench. But Tom and Frank were seniors — and confident enough in their talents to ask for a bit of independence. Could they, the pair inquired, call some of their own plays? To which Ara replied:

"Nope."

"I'll tell you why I call all the plays," he said. "I've worked a long time to get where I am. And I'm not going to have some nineteen-year-old kid messing it up for me."

★   ★   ★

"Tell you what a difference Ara made around here," observed a stadium security guard shortly after the coach's retirement. "When he was coaching not a soul stayed out in the parking lot. When Kuharich was here, we'd have a slew of people at tailgate parties that'd run right through the game."

★   ★   ★

Parseghian made pep rallies popular again.

XII.
Monumental Myths

Washington Hall, so the legend goes, is the home of George Gipp's ghost. They say that after a late night on the town Gipp slept on the steps of the building and picked up the infection that led to his death. His spirit returned to the place because it housed a pool table, the most alluring item in his life. Somewhere in the dusty darkness of the century-old structure, The Gipper's phantom lurks, chalking its cue, looking for a game.

★   ★   ★

A statue of Father William Corby stands under a tree in front of the building bearing his name. Corby is portrayed with his right hand poised in the air. The statue is called — what else? — "Fair Catch" Corby.

Years from now, somewhere on campus, Father Hesburgh's image will probably be commemorated in stone, his arms outstretched, to be called — what else? — "TV Time-Out" Teddy.

★   ★   ★

And if there was ever any doubt in the minds of Notre Dame fans just who is number one, a gigantic Moses stands hard by the library as heavenly support.

Joseph Turkalj, who had deeper imagery in mind when he sculpted the statue, doesn't really mind that people think Moses is proclaiming the football team's national ranking: "You have to expect that on the Notre Dame campus," he says. "But I look at it this way: at least people are still talking about the statue."

★   ★   ★

When the Notre Dame Library was completed in 1964, the administration rolled out stacks of publicity on the value of the building to the school's academic life.

Then it was discovered that a football player waiting to receive a kick-off in the south end of the stadium could see the mosaic on the face of the library: Jesus with this arms upraised. Cynics speculated that the library was nothing more than an edifice hex, an eight million dollar psych job to deflate visiting teams. "Touchdown Jesus" was the name given the artwork.

It's got to be an unnerving sight for opponents: The Great Referee peeking over the scoreboard, reminding them that Notre Dame is worth six points before the opening kick.

★ ★ ★

XIII.
Green Machine
1975- _____

A flashback of mid-seventies nostalgia:

Space shuttles, Sun Myung Moonies, Tongsun Park, a new Yankee Stadium. Patty Hearst, Bert Lance, Dr. J., Billy Beer. Innocent days when you didn't know Plains, Georgia, or Kepone existed.

Every Winter was the worst winter in history. Ronald Reagan ran for president; Gipp wouldnt have liked the odds. America's top cop, J. Edgar Hoover, became a national disgrace.

So long, Panama Canal. So long, gas wars, diamond lanes, and Mayor Daley. So long, Bing and Groucho and Elvis.

Hello *Roots,* disco, CB radios.

And hello, Dan Devine.

★   ★   ★

Back before the beginning of the 1960 season when Dan Devine was coaching the University of Missouri, he became terribly preoccupied with his team's chances for the fall. Mrs. Jo Devine was eagerly anticipating the birth of their fifth child, but the expectant father was preparing for an opening game. You know what wins out in a football household.

"Just think, Dan," said Jo one day, obviously referring to the imminent arrrival of a newborn Devine, "it's less than a month to go now."

"I know," said the brooding coach, "and already three starters out with injuries."

★   ★   ★

Devine began to address the team. As always, his voice was soft, a librarian's voice. He mentioned the importance of the first game without indulging in specifics: the first game of the season; the first ever against Boston College; the first of his coaching career at Notre Dame. He touched upon the importance of the Notre Dame family, then he was through. It was a low-key but effective pep talk that soothed the worst of everybody's pre-game jitters.

Then, smoothly, Devine switched to strategy, naming the plays the offense would run on its first series. The players watched closely and blinked at one another with increasingly puzzled expressions. The coach was using strange and unfamiliar terminology. Who could understand what was being said? From the looks of things, no one but Dan Devine.

An assistant walked up and whispered to his boss and Devine was suddenly back with the program, ticking off plays his team had been practicing for weeks. What happened? The coach's calm exterior had belied a tension probably worse than any of his boys'. He had been naming offensive sets from his days as Green Bay Packer coach, plays not even included in the Notre Dame playbook!

Even then, Devine must have been preoccupied with the wearing of the green and gold.

★   ★   ★

Scheduling is the reigning absurdity of college football. If you remember back to the days of Jesse Harper and before, it was common practice for the fall slate to be chalked up a mere six months in advance. Rockne, with characteristic efficiency, was filling his football calendar two and three years ahead by the time of this death. Layden went Rock a year or two better. By the mid-fifties, Notre Dame was scheduling six years into the future, as were all colleges.

Abnormal psychologists can best explain why a few institutions were driven to break out of the six year pattern and schedule eight years ahead.

Whatever the reason, every other school followed suit: mob reaction by major American universities. From six years to eight to ten, the cycle spiraled to idiotic heights. As of this printing, Notre Dame is scheduled sixteen to twenty seasons ahead.

Too often, the price of such foolishness is good competition. Take, for example, the University of Pittsburgh's untimely disappearance from the Notre Dame schedule. By the late sixties, the long rivalry had become an embarrassment to both schools. Between 1965 and 1969 the Panthers lost to the Irish by a combined score of 252-27. Notre Dame was criticized for scheduling a patsy. Pitt seemed on the unswervable path of football de-emphasis, and did not require a yearly humiliation by a clearly superior team.

So the schools amicably agreed to end the series. We need hardly bother noting that within a few short seasons Pitt's football fortunes experienced a dramatic rebirth. Walloping Notre Dame in 1975 and 1976, the Panthers capped their stunning comeback with a well-earned national championship. The old rivalry was big-time football once more, but it was too late to patch up the separation.

A series renewal is being anxiously plotted; it should take place somewhere around the turn of the century.

★   ★   ★

Father Jerome Wilson, Notre Dame's vice president for business affairs, was trotting across campus one spring afternoon when he spotted Walter Miller, a fullback from the days of Jesse Harper and Knute Rockne. Let Father Wilson tell the story:

I could tell it was Walter right away, because he

was dressed completely in white. He had a strong affection for that color. I never saw him when he wasn't dressed in a white suit, white socks and shoes, white shirt and hat. You could always pick him out in the stands at a football game because he wore a heavy white overcoat. Oh, it's a beautiful coat, very warm. It's hanging upstairs in my closet right now. But we'll get to that later.

How much did Walter Miller like white? He always drove a white Cadillac with a white interior. The color was his trademark.

Anyway, I had seen Walter back on campus for years, usually in the lobby of the Morris Inn. He was easy to notice. But I always was too busy to say much to him. "Hello, Walter," I'd say. "You're looking great. I wish I could stay and talk, but I have to get upstairs to a meeting."

So this day I was heading across campus to another meeting. And I saw Walter, all by himself, standing in front of the LaFortune Student Center.

I said to myself: Wilson, go over and say hello. We had a warm handshake, but this time Walter didn't even let me tell him how good he was looking. He had a troubled expression.

"You know, Father," he said. "I was just standing here thinking. No one loves football more than I do. And from where I sit in the stands, I can't even see the field. My eyes are that bad."

I felt so sorry for Walter I said: "Leave it to me. I am going to get you two seats, four rows up, on the fifty yard line."

I had no idea where I would get the tickets . . . but I was determined.

It made Walter very happy. "If you only could, Father," he said. "I'd just love to be able to see the game again."

★

So I searched all that summer and finally found

those tickets for Walter. And I sent them off to him. At the beginning of the season, I saw him in the lobby of the Morris Inn.

"Father," he said, "the seats you got me are wonderful. I want you to step outside. I have something for you."

That something was a pure white Cadillac.

"It's yours, Father."

"Walter, I can't take it."

He shook his head.

"I think, Walter, you know the rules of the Order. I can't accept a car for myself. But if you want to give it to the University, I'll gladly accept it — but I want you to know that we'll probably just sell it."

"Do whatever you want, Father Wilson. The car is yours, with my thanks."

★

That was one of the last times I saw Walter. I got the tickets for him next season, but he was too sick to use them. About six months later, I got a call from his brother, Don. [Note: Don Miller, of the Four Horsemen.]

Don said: "Father, I have unhappy news and good news. The sad news is that Walter has passed away after that long illness. The good news is that he remembered you in his will. You get two thousand dollars, to travel."

"Don, I can't take the money unless my provincial gives me permission."

"Father, Walter left specific instructions that this money was for you to travel with. Don't worry about the Order. He made sure that the University was well taken care of. I'm a judge and a lawyer and dollars, the bequest to the University will not be made."

dollars, the bequest to the university will not be made."

So, with my superior's permission, I accepted. Don gave me some of Walter's clothes, besides, including that topcoat. That winter I used Walter's bequest to visit Israel, Athens, and Rome. Oh, let me tell you, it was a delightful trip.

I made out pretty well. For getting Walter Miller those tickets worth about a hundred dollars — which he paid for anyway — the University got a Cadillac, and I got a trip to the Mediterranean and part of an all-white wardrobe.

I still get those tickets every year, and I look all around the campus for another Walter Miller: someone dressed all in white.

★ ★ ★

The hardhats at Commonwealth Edison in Joliet, Illinois, where Dan "Rudy" Reuttiger worked used to think it was a laugh: their little five-foot six, college dropout, Navy veteran buddy had ambitions not only to attend Notre Dame — he was going to play football for the Fighting Irish. "Forget it, Rudy," the hardhats would cluck. "The guys on that team buff their shoes with guys like you. Maybe they'll let you be the leprechaun."

Certainly it was a far-fetched dream. No one seemed to think Rudy Reuttiger could get into Notre Dame. And anyone who thought he'd wind up playing for the Irish . . . well, those people had special rooms in state-run institutions.

But see for yourself:

Deep down on the 1975 Notre Dame roster Dan Reuttiger's name appears. He actually made it. A halfhearted semester of college, two years in the Navy and a couple more on Conn Ed's payroll came first — but he made it. "It was always a dream of mine, buddy," says the vet from Joliet. "I knew I could do it." That statement speaks Rudy Reuttiger's creed: believe you can do anything, and address everyone as "buddy."

Rudy shored up his dismal academic record with two years at a junior college. In the fall of 1974, a twenty-six year-old junior, he was admitted to Notre Dame.

And like all students with sound life insurance policies he was permitted to walk on for football. At five-six, 170 pounds, Reuttiger was Notre Dame's unlikeliest defensive lineman in half a century. He compensated with a gung-ho style that might be described as "Saturday Night in a Shanghai Saloon": pinballed all over the field by the varsity, he would eagerly toe the line for more. "Rudy had a great attitude," says Defensive Coach Joe Yonto. "He'd play anywhere, and he wasn't afraid to stick people. We'd put him in whenever the preppers needed somebody on defense."

But suiting up for a daily pummeling from the Big Guys and playing in a varsity game are two different matters. When the NCAA limited to sixty the number of players allowed to dress for home games, Reuttiger's slim chance to see action in 1975, his senior season, had seemingly been snuffed. He was nowhere near the top sixty. He was way, way down on the depth chart. Down so deep he'd have to decompress if he ever came up.

But tenacity was his specialty. Before the final home game of the season against Georgia Tech, he marched into the football office and, in no uncertain terms, delivered his message to the coaches: he had to dress for that game. It was his lifelong ambition to play for the Irish. How could he play, he asked, if he wasn't in uniform?

Devine listened. "Rudy was an inspiration to the team," he says. "More than anyone else he deserved to dress for Georgia Tech. We put his name on the list."

Could this have anything but a happy ending? On Saturday the Irish built a lead that stood solid through the fourth quarter. Reuttiger agonized on the bench. With thirty seconds in the game Tech got the ball; Rudy got the call. He hitched up his pants, chugged out to the huddle, and heard the stadium announcer blare what he had waited twenty-seven years for: "Reuttiger in for Notre Dame!"

The team, which normally watched the ends of lopsided games with placid disinterest, hugged the sidelines and cheered. Rudy dug in at defensive end. On the final play of the game — possibly by darting between the offensive lineman's legs — he broke clean. He swung in like a wrecking ball and toppled the quarterback. A sack!

A knot of grinning, whooping teammates heaved him to their shoulders and gave him a hero's ride off the field. He hadn't dramatically won a game, or wasted some long-standing record. But Rudy Reuttiger's victory was easily the most important of the day.

★ ★ ★

When Joe Restic, son of the Harvard football coach, was asked why he didn't attend Harvard and play under his father, Trainer Gene Paszkiet was quick with the answer: "Because he didn't want to go to a football factory."

★ ★ ★

Their two previous meetings had been decided by a total of three points. Now, for the third time in three years, the Irish and Alabama had each other by the throat. At the end of the first quarter there was no score and everything pointed to another gut-wrenching game.

In a game like this you expect a team —

especially a team with an active defense like Notre Dame's — to be conservative. Force a fumble. Block a punt. Squeeze them till they crack.

But Dan Devine likes surprises. He had watched the Crimson Tide defense cheat tighter and tighter against the run; the defensive backs were almost at the line of scrimmage. Any coach knows that the time to throw long is when the Tide is in. Devine decided to try a long pass straight off.

As the coach paced nervously waiting for the second quarter to begin, he spied Father James Riehle, the team chaplain. On game days Riehle wears a houndstooth hat and keeps a cigar wedged into a corner of his mouth, looking for all the world

The Cigar and Father Jim.

like a bookie in a Roman collar. "How about a prayer, Father," smiled Devine. "We're going for the bomb on the first play."

In view of the offense's impotency in earlier games Father Riehle probably said a prayer to St. Jude, the patron of lost causes. But St. Jude came through, as did Rick Slager and Dan Kelleher, who hooked up on a 56-yard touchdown pass. The Irish were off and not running.

Father Riehle prides himself in his work. After the completion he sought out Devine. "How's *that* for a prayer, coach?" he asked, flicking a bit of ash from his cigar.

"Stay right where you are, Father," said the coach, a man who knows talent when he sees it. "We may need you later in the game."

Fighting Irish fans can rest easy. Riehle intends to stay at Notre Dame for the rest of his praying days.

★ ★ ★

Dan Devine, in reference to some of the alumni who persisted in attacks on his character: "It's not so bad. Last week a group of Chicago alumni presented me with a pair of moccasins. Water moccasins."

★ ★ ★

Devine had gotten the idea from a letter amidst the huge stack of mail waiting on his desk his first day at Notre Dame: a former student manager under Frank Leahy wanted to see the Irish wear green again. The new coach was intrigued by the notion and kept it in mind. Two-and-a-half years later he would use it with maximum possible effect.

In 1977 Notre Dame was facing a mid-season crisis with Southern Cal. After a sputtering start

Dan Devine — no longer blue.

the team had shown signs of life, and the game with the Trojans loomed as an acid test. As he does before all big games, Devine looked for a psychological sword.

He had called Willie Fry, one of the captains, into his office several weeks earlier and asked how he'd feel about changing to green jerseys. Fry had been lukewarm to the idea. ("I thought the man had gone over the edge," he recalled later. "I tried, but I just couldn't picture us in green.") But Devine had gone ahead with his plan. On the Wednesday before USC he invited Fry, Steve Orsini and Terry Eurick — the other two captains — to the football auditorium. When the trio arrived Ross Browner was on stage, modeling the most fantastic green and gold football get-up they had ever seen. Their glee was unbridled. (Willie Fry: "I said, 'Bring on USC!' I wanted to play them right there.") The coach huddled with the four players and told them of his scheme. They vowed to keep it a secret.

After Friday's practice Irish Tennis Coach Tom Fallon serenaded the team in its dressing room with a number of Irish ballads, among them *The Wearin' of the Green.* Then Devine spoke to the players of the torments suffered in years past by the Irish people. He spoke of their fierce pride. he told them what it meant to wear green during the Black and Tan oppression. And he reminded them of their own proud ethnic backgrounds, that their ancestors, like the Irish, had to fight for their beliefs. It was a speech that would gain significance the next day.

That night at the pep rally Fry urged all the fans to wear green to the game. Basketball coach Digger Phelps did the same, and concluded his speech by whipping the crowd into a chant of "Green Machine! Green Machine!" Some of the fans looked a mite puzzled, but the players were too busy with thoughts of the Trojans to make any deductions.

Saturday . . . . Before the game warm-ups were taken in the standard blue jerseys. Only when the players returned to the locker room ten minutes before kick-off did they see the new uniforms hanging in their stalls. The discovery touched off a celebration. "Like kids on Christmas morning," is the way one coach described it. The cheer of the night before made sense now, and the team picked it up: "Green Machine! Green Machine! Green Machine! . . ."

GREEN MACHINE

And when the sartorially splendid Irish stormed the field . . . well, there's only one way to describe fan reaction: 59,075 people turned simultaneously to the person next to them and shouted, "They're wearing *green!*"

"I saw them come out screaming in those jerseys," said USC linebacker Clay Matthews, "and I knew we were in trouble." And indeed they were. If the Irish had come out pulling howitzers the Trojans wouldn't have been more surprised — or more defenseless. They were stymied at every turn. Linebacker Bob Golic jammed up the middle on defense. Joe Montana stoked the offense to full throttle. And Ted Burgmeier was underfoot all day long.

The five-ten cornerback bedeviled the Trojans by: returning an interception thirty-eight yards with a classic broken-field run; running a faked field goal attempt for a key first down; again from his position as holder turning a muffed snap from center into a two-point conversion by sprinting wide and dinking a short pass to Tom Domin; and making eight tackles. Folks in the stands were pulling hamstrings just from watching Ted go.

The final score of 49 to 19 was just about the size of it. The Irish struck a dizzying emotional peak before the game and would have steamrolled anyone in their way. USC was the unlucky victim. For the first time that season, Notre Dame realized its awesome potential. And why not? It was easy wearing green.

★   ★   ★

Usually cool under pressure, Dan Devine was just plain cold the night before the Clemson game. Sometime between midnight and dawn there was a knock on his door at the Holiday Inn-Clemson. It was Joe O'Brien, Notre Dame's business manager.

Ted Burgmeier vs. USC: to hold or not to hold?

"Coach," said O'Brien, "I've just talked with the manager. He got a call saying there's a bomb in your room. You think we should evacuate the hotel?"

"There's no bomb in here," mumbled Devine. "I know. I've been up half the night just looking for an extra blanket."

★   ★   ★

For as many quarterbacks as he yanked down by the shirttail in his career, Ross Browner sure had a devil of a time holding onto his own uniform. He lost one on a flight to Los Angeles to tape a Kodak TV special. The producers scrambled and put together a reasonable facsimile of a Fighting Irish outfit. It was a mite tight, of course, which explains why Ross wore an odd expression through the telecast. That was the look of a man afraid to exhale.

Another of his uniforms disappeared after the 1977 Miami game. No sooner was it loaded into the luggage compartment of the team bus than a light-fingered youngster boosted it out the opposite side.

Anyone seeing a short Miamian with a pair of shoulder pads roughly the size of Cuba is asked to call the Notre Dame Athletic Department.

★   ★   ★

If you were in Dallas for the 1978 Cotton Bowl to see the Irish clinch the 1977 National Championship, you may have noticed the priest sitting near the thirty-five yard line. He held a Notre Dame pennant in one hand and a Texas banner in the other. Each time Irish scored, the Notre Dame pennant received a slight wave. When Texas so much as moved the ball an inch, the Longhorn banner was thrust high and twirled like a top.

Explained the Reverend Father: "I've been a

Holy Cross priest for ten years, but a Texan all my life."

★ ★ ★

In 1913, Jesse Harper scratched and cajoled, and finally got the Army to pay Notre Dame a thousand dollars for a football game.

In April of 1978, Notre Dame received its revenues from January's Cotton Bowl. The sum: a cool $1,008,371.92.

Green? Gold? Appropriate.

★ ★ ★ ★ ★ ★ ★ ★ ★ ★ ★ ★ ★

XIV.
The Notre Dame Dream Game

Of course your choices will differ, but here are our picks for Notre Dame's All-Time Team.

Coach: Knute Rockne

Offense	Defense
QB-Frank Carideo (1930)	DB-John Lujack (1947)
RB-Creighton Miller (1943)	DB-Luther Bradley (1977)
RB-George Gipp (1920)	DB-Johnny Lattner (1953)
RB-Paul Hornung (1956)	LB-Red Salmon (1903)
C-Adam Walsh (1924)	LB-Jim Lynch (1966)
G-Bill Fischer (1948)	LB-Nick Buoniconti (1961)
G-Tom Regner (1966)	DL-Ross Browner (1977)
T-Jim White (1943)	DL-George Connor (1947)
T-Joe Kurth (1932)	DL-Hunk Anderson (1921)
TE-Dave Casper (1973)	DL-Frank Rydzewski (1917)
WR-Tom Gatewood (1971)	DL-Leon Hart (1949)

(Final season in parentheses)

Pit them against the people who have damaged the Irish most over the years: All-Time All-Star Opponents.

Coach: John McKay

Offense	Defense
QB-Mike Phipps (Purdue 1969)	DB-Herb Adderly (MSU 1960)
RB-Kyle Rote (SMU 1951)	DB-Billy Vessels (Okla. 1952)
RB-Anthony Davis (USC 1974)	DB-Doc Blanchard (Army 1946)
RB-Marshall Goldberg (Pitt 1938)	LB-James Sims (USC 1973)
C-Gomer Jones (Ohio State 1935)	LB-Elmer Q. Oliphant (Army 1916)
G-Bill Daddio (Pitt 1938)	LB-Nile Kinnick (Iowa 1939)
G-Gary Roberts (Purdue 1968)	DL-Bubba Smith (MSU 1966)
T-Lloyd Yoder (Carnegie Tech 1926)	DL-Ed Wier (Nebr. 1925)
T-John Vella (USC 1971)	DL-Alex Karras (Iowa 1957)
TE-Mike Ditka (Pitt 1960)	DL-Ralph Capwell (Marquette 1911)
WR-Johnny Rodgers (Nebr. 1972)	DL-Dick Duden (Navy 1945)

(School and final season in parentheses)

★   ★   ★

★   ★   ★

Throw in the All-Time Cheerleading Squads, Marching Bands, and Mascots.

	Notre Dame	Opponent
Cheerleaders:	1971 squad (led by Terri Buck)	1975 USC Song Girls
Band:	1887 Fifin' Irish (on hand for the first Notre Dame game)	1971 MSU Spartan Marching Band
Mascot:	Clashmore Mike I	Beavo, the Texas Steer

All-Time Site: Soldier Field, c. 1930
(Attendance: 120,000)

★   ★   ★   ★   ★   ★

This speculation has gone so far that we might as well make it a football game. With sincerest apologies to Damon Runyon, our All-Time Sportswriter, here is an account . . .

★   ★   ★   ★   ★   ★

"**W**e don't have a crowd this big in years and years," remarks one of your all-time Andy Frain ushers as he gawks at the 120,000 expectant souls packing the stands in Soldier Field. But then they do not have a game this big in years and years.

Outside the specs are lining their pockets, so to speak, as they are getting fifty dollars a ducket from the innocents who dearly want to see this game. These duckets are five dollars for those who buy them in advance — a costly lesson for fans who are paying fifty dollars for a seat that is halfway to Gary, Indiana.

The faithful wade into this monstrous edifice, and they gasp when they see the athletes who are down on the field breaking a sweat: Lujack, Rote, Blanchard and Davis (this one Anthony), Hart, Browner, and that Karras fellow, who is this reporter's favorite for spinning funny but unprintable stories. The crowd is oohing and ahhing and thousands of fingers point out their favorites.

Meanwhile Coaches Rockne and McKay stand on the sidelines and discuss the game they are going to direct.

"I am hoping your boys take it easy on us today," says Rockne, who is always looking to soften up the other fellow. "We have not had much time to practice."

"Listen to him," laughs McKay. "Just like a fox trying to talk his way into the henhouse."

"If those are hens," says Rockne, as he nods in the direction of Smith and Vella, "there is not a fox on this earth that stands a chance."

★   ★   ★

The All-Stars win the toss and choose to receive.

Gipp floats a kick deep to the dangerous Mr. Davis, who waits in the end zone and muffs the catch. He tries to snatch the elusive pigskin while the crowd roars, but he makes the wise choice of downing the ball when he hears the hoofbeats of the Notre Dame eleven. The All-Time Opponents begin from the twenty.

It is feared that the game will not be played for keeps, but this notion is allayed on the first play when Salmon hits Goldberg with a blow that rattles typewriters in the press box.

The teams play a chess game for the first six minutes. Three times the ball is exchanged on punts. Then from the T-formation Carideo tries a quick forward pass to Gatewood. Smith gets a big paw up and deflects the ball. Blanchard springs up to make the interception at the Notre Dame forty and runs the ball to the eighteen.

From there it is only academic for Mr. Phipps. He gives to Davis for six. He passes to Ditka, who outfights Bradley and Lujack at the two. Then Goldberg bucks across the right tackle for the score. After Kinnick converts, the All-Time Opponents lead 7 to nothing at 7:22 of the quarter.

★   ★   ★

The score does not stay like that long, however, which relieves my friend, the renowned German Herbie, who takes the side of Notre Dame and stakes a healthy bite of his yearly wage on the outcome. "It is a lock cinch," says German Herbie before the game, but then he sees the likes of Capwell and Sims, and wonders if he has made a mistake.

★   ★   ★

White and Fischer begin to hold sway in the line. Gipp and Miller get running room, and between them they carry the mail to the fifteen. Elmer Q. Oliphant stops Miller for no gain on third down, and the Irishmen have to content themselves with a field goal. The quarter ends with the score at 7 to 3.

★   ★   ★

No one ever sees a better demonstration of offensive football than what goes on in the second quarter.

Phipps starts it off by chucking an aerial to Rodgers, who leaves Lattner counting his change at the 26-yard line, and advances the ball to the mid-stripe. Out of a pro set, Phipps wants to pass again, but the greeting committee of Rydzewski and Browner waits for him in the backfield. So for the rest of the way, Rote and Goldberg lug the melon, mixing spinner plays and off-tackle runs from a T. The All-Time Opponents forge to the thirty, but then Connor, Anderson, and Rydzewski give no more in the middle. Buoniconti breaks up a pass that Rote aims at Rodgers. Kinnick boots a 47-yard field goal, and the score is 10 to 3.

The Fighting Irishmen come out with a furious campaign of their own, which starts when Hornung returns the kick-off to the 37. Carideo begins to work his sleight-of-hand, and catches the opponents' line leaning the wrong way with some slick ball handling out of the Notre Dame shift. Adderly comes within a hairbreadth of making the score 16 to 3, as he is in position to intercept a Hornung pass with an open field ahead. But Casper bats the ball into the air and catches it as he falls to

the sod at the opponents' 38. Casper's pip of a catch brings the crowd roaring to its feet.

Carideo has the defense back on its haunches, and he deploys his troops strategically. Notre Dame presently grinds out two more first downs to the twenty: Gipp gets eight around right end; Hornung slips trying to reach a Carideo pass, but Carideo tries it again, and this time they make the connection for nine yards. On a third down from the sixteen Hornung chucks a beauty to Gatewood for the score. Gipp's point is true. The score is 10 to 10 with 5:18 left on the timer.

The next time the Stars have the ball Browner is very much surprised when he is presented with a gift, namely a fumble by Phipps. Anderson sneaks up behind the quarterback when he is looking to pass, raps him sharply, and forces him to drop the ball.

Notre Dame takes over on the thirty. They move twenty yards on three lugs by Miller, and a Carideo to Gatewood pass. The drive stalls. Gipp boots a field goal into the wind. The Fighting Irish fight to their first lead of the game, 13 to 10.

★   ★   ★

Irish fans celebrate noisily in the stands. His financial status looking up, German Herbie takes large nips of an amber-colored fluid. When Notre Dame shows promise, the German swings his coat above his head like he is a helicopter trying to take off.

★   ★   ★

No sooner do 120,000 settle back than the Stars are on the march. Rote catches a third-down chuck from Phipps and hauls it for twelve. Goldberg pounds inside and Davis gets loose for some occasional acreage outside, and the Stars chew up forty yards. A pass falls incomplete. The next play is a pass, too, and Bradley is whistled for interfering with Ditka at the Irish twenty-five. The South Bend bench complains, but to no avail.

Rote plugs for four to the Notre Dame 21-yard line. Goldberg rifles through the line for ten before Lynch neckties him. With less than a minute in the half, the All-Time Opponents cover the distance to the goal on four quick bucks. Goldberg rides in on Roberts' shank from the two. Hart stampedes in to block the kick, and the half ends with the Stars ahead 16 to 13.

★   ★   ★

Kinnick boots to Hornung to start the second half. Hornung runs to the eighteen, where he fumbles but leaps out and snatches the ball an instant before Duden jacknifes onto it.

With the wind at their backs the Fighting Irish go from the T-formation and plow for three first downs. When Wier stops Gipp on third down they are forced into a Carideo punt.

The opponents find no success however, and must boot the melon right back.

Both defenses shine. Connor and Browner repeatedly play havoc with All-Time All-Star Opponent blockers; Lujack is the surest tackler on the field. The opponents are just as stingy: Capwell and Karras are full of fight; Adderly and Blanchard both play the game sideline to sideline.

Rote poses a threat halfway through the quarter when he rambles for fourteen, and then Goldberg tacks on nine more. On fourth-and-one from the Notre Dame 35-yard line, the Stars decide to gamble for a first down. Goldberg fails to gain when

he is smacked by Buoniconti in a collision that is heard all over the joint.

Notre Dame takes over, but the rest of the period is spent in a cautious punting exchange. "Death Hole" Carideo keeps his team in good field position with some lovely kicking into the corners, but the South Benders cannot profit from this propitious situation. The quarter ends with the count still 16 to 13.

★   ★   ★

All of which is making the venerable German Herbie quite anxious. He is saying that he sweats through horse races, cock fights, boxing matches, and church bingos, but he never sweats like this before. This is because he never before makes a bet of this magnitude. If German Herbie loses the bet, a certain Sammy the Sleeve, who lives in Queens, New York, will own German Herbie's house, his car, and two of his children.

★   ★   ★

With two minutes gone in the final stanza Notre Dame mounts an offensive that begins on their own thirty-five. Miller skips around right end for six. Gipp rides a block from Kurth to the forty-nine. Gipp is stopped twice by the left side of the All-Star line, but Casper gets ground to spare when he gathers in a neat flip from Hornung on a lateral pass. Notre Dame is penalized five yards. When Gipp tries to get that and a little extra back with a toss to Hornung, Vessels swoops in and intercepts on the twelve-yard line.

The next play by the Stars has everybody in the joint on his feet. Phipps lobs a little five yard pass to Ditka, and when Bradley and Salmon hit the latter from behind he laterals the ball to Rodgers, who

heads toward Union Station. Only an ankle grab by Lujack keeps the speedy Rodgers from catching his train. He gains sixty-six yards on the play.

Three plays later Rote pokes his noggin through a hole in the line for the score. Kinnick's boot is wide, and the count stands 22 to 13 with a little over eight minutes remaining.

★   ★   ★

German Herbie makes his way onto the side-lines and wanders quite aimlessly, a bottle in his hand.

★   ★   ★

After taking the kick-off, Notre Dame drives into the wind. The firm of White, Fischer, Walsh, Regner, Kurth and Casper rolls up its sleeves and goes to work. Hornung takes a pitch-out and picks up seven, then hammers through center for six more. Carideo surprises with a bootleg out of the I for nine and a first down. Then Gipp powers his way off left tackle for twenty-two yards in four lugs of the old melon. Wier drops Carideo for a loss. But the latter gets the real estate back with a screen to Hornung, who walks a tight-rope past the All-Star bench for eighteen. The rest of the drive is effective but time-consuming. Miller tunnels for three. Hornung is stopped by tall Bubba Smith, but Miller comes back to rip off seven for a first down at the All-Star twelve. Three cracks by Miller precede a one yard plunge by Mr. Hornung. Gipp adds the point-after. With 4:20 left in the game the score stands at 22 to 20. 120,000 stand on their feet for the finish.

And what a finish it is! Notre Dame kicks away, and for an instant it looks as if Davis has an opening as he cuts into the clear at the thirty-five. But he runs into big Leon Hart, which is the same as butting your head against the Statue of Liberty, and he is downed on the spot.

The All-Stars try to bleed the clock. They run little cross bucks off the rear ends of Vella and Daddio, who have done yeoman work all day. Goldberg and Rote pick up two, three and four yards at a crack. With two minutes and thirty-eight seconds left in the game, the All-Stars have a second and eight at their own forty-eight yard line. Yoder is whistled for offsides. Notre Dame holds for two downs on fine tackles by Hart and Connor. The Stars, only one first down from salting away the game, have to kick.

The Fighting Irish use their last time-out with exactly two minutes showing on the clock.

★ ★ ★

Unable to take the strain, German Herbie decides to take a little nap near the 20-yard line marker. No one pays any attention to him except Clashmore Mike, a dog who earns his keep as Notre Dame's mascot. Clashmore Mike gnaws and tugs on one of German Herbie's ears.

★ ★ ★

Lattner is put into the game to receive Rote's punt. He gathers it on the twenty, gives Elmer Q. Oliphant the limp leg, and runs the pigskin to the forty-one. Notre Dame hurries its offense, running from the shift. With 1:38 remaining Gipp chucks a ten yard pass to Miller.

Carideo lofts one out of bounds, stopping the clock at 1:12. The huge crowd is howling now. The noise does not let up, even between plays.

Notre Dame advances the ball to the All-Star thirty-six on two Hornung-to-Gatewood sideline passes. But only fifty seconds show on the timer, and against the wind they are out of field goal range.

Two forward passes fall incomplete, leaving just thirty-three seconds in the game. The players can barely hear Carideo's count through the din.

Not one of the assembled multitude believes what he sees next.

Hornung takes a direct snap from center and looks to Gatewood, who is shadowed by Adderly on the sidelines. He wings the ball down the middle to Casper. The latter makes the catch at the nineteen, but he fails to get out of bounds, and the clock is ticking down from twenty seconds.

The Irish dash down and line up for a field goal. Naturally the All-Time All-Star Opponents take their time assuming their positions, so the ref stops the clock with three seconds left.

Then everything is happening at once: the referee whips his arm in a circle to start the timer; the clock ticks from one to zero just as the ball is snapped; the lines lock for one last time; and the errant snap sails crazily over the holder Carideo's head, and past the kicker Gipp.

There is an explosion from the All-Star Partisans, who know that their boys are assured a victory.

But Gipp knows that the contest is not yet finished. He chases down the ball and fetches it on the 30-yard line, and circles wide to avoid the grasp of Smith. For a breathless instant it appears he might have an alley to the goal line, but Sims and Blanchard dash over to close it off.

Gipp doubles back and sprints to the twenty-four, where he gets a brief opening and lets loose with a drop-kick. It is a high, fluttering shot into the wind. 120,000 fans watch the ball travel its course. Gipp is the first to see that the ball's flight takes it

through the uprights. He turns to where Rockne and the others are standing on the sidelines, his arms upraised, and shouts, "That one is for me, Rock!"

Then there is pandemonium in Soldier Field, as Notre Dame fans storm the gridiron.

★ ★ ★

Some days later this reporter sees the esteemed German Herbie on the street. He smokes a dollar cigar and wears a big gauze bandage on his left ear. "It pays," he says with a puff of smoke, "to know a sure thing when you see it."

★ ★ ★

The End